The Post-Pandemic Law Firm

EDITED BY ALEX DAVIES

Commissioning editor
Alex Davies

Managing director
Sian O'Neill

The Post-Pandemic Law Firm is published by

Globe Law and Business Ltd
3 Mylor Close
Horsell
Woking
Surrey GU21 4DD
United Kingdom
Tel: +44 20 3745 4770
www.globelawandbusiness.com

The Post-Pandemic Law Firm

ISBN 9781787428010
EPUB ISBN 9781787428027
Adobe PDF ISBN 9781787428034

Contents

Executive summary

Over a year has passed since the beginning of the COVID-19 pandemic and with vaccine rollouts and dipping numbers of COVID-19 cases, the world is beginning to reopen. Regardless, the pandemic has seemingly had a lasting impact on how business is conducted and the modern law firm is not immune. In fact, the pandemic merely expedited changes that were already trending – flexible work schedules, fully-remote offices, revised resource allocations, new client expectations, and even casual wear while working. These changes are not only here to stay but have become the expectation. Law firm attorneys and staff are no longer interested in a traditional office. Gone is the requirement of decorum. Clients seldom need or want to sit in an office to discuss their case. The modern law firm needs to evolve with both employee and consumer expectations in order to stay abreast with the post-pandemic world. This opening chapter by Wayne Hassay of Maguire Schneider Hassay, LLP explains the issues.

In chapter two, John Chisholm takes a look at some of the effects the COVID-19 pandemic has had on law firms and posits that the pandemic made firms adopt practices, methodologies, and strategies that pre-COVID they insisted they could not. John queries whether such new practices are only reactive and temporary or whether some are here to stay and will become embedded into the structure and culture of firms. The chapter looks at whether now is the time that law firms should make a paradigm shift and adopt an entirely new business model that externally focuses on providing outcomes, outputs, and results to their clients and internally places the wellbeing of their team as a cornerstone to the future long-term success and sustainability of the legal profession.

In the waning months of the devastating Second World War, as world leaders were looking toward a post-war future, Winston Churchill expounded these leaders to create the UN. His call to action was characterized by a famous quote, *"Never let a good crisis go to waste"*. The eventual recognition that in the wake of war there was an opportunity to embrace change in a manner that would have previously unthinkable, resulted in the UN and one of the longest periods of economic growth, the expansion of human rights, and overall global prosperity.

COVID-19 has, without question, created global economic devastation and human misery not seen since the Second World War. But similarly to the opportunity identified by Churchill, global leaders have an opportunity to harness many of the changes forced upon them to create a new positive future. The legal profession has an opportunity to be one of those industries that picks up positives from this pandemic and makes changes that not only improve the delivery of legal services, but also improves the working conditions of lawyers and professionals as well as delivering greater profitability. The restrictions and lockdowns that have characterized the COVID-19 pandemic have been a time of great stress and dislocation, and for far too many a period of huge loss. Consequently, there is a deep desire to go back to "normal" to "the way it was before". For those law firms leaders and lawyers that realize a return to normal is exactly the wrong approach, says Stuart Wilson of BIRA in chapter three, there is an opportunity to create a brighter future where work–life balance, market innovation, and smart use of technology will define the law firm of the future.

This potential for law firms to improve both internally and externally is expounded upon by Patricia Gillette in chapter four. We need women in law firm leadership now more than ever – but firms must reflect on how COVID-19 has influenced the profession over the last 18 months, in order to take a long-term look at life in a law firm. As we have learned from the pandemic, careers can ebb and flow due to personal and professional circumstances. Law firms need to recognize that women in particular experience limits and constraints in time and energy at points in their careers and come up with ways to create a working lifecycle that takes these peaks and troughs into account.

Reduced to the most elementary definition, law firms are business entities formed by one or more lawyers to engage in the practice of law. In the legal industry, clients continue to demand more for less, workers demand more work–life harmony, regulation around the practice of law is changing, technology allows us to work smarter, not harder, and our market reach is expanding. For these reasons, we are at a juncture where we can have viable business models of legal service delivery that go beyond the traditional law firm model. In chapter five, Yvonne Nath of LawVision and ALSP Advisor discusses some of these emerging and potential business models for law firms and other law companies, how they challenge the status quo, who they serve, and how they can succeed.

Continuing this theme, Mary Juetten, co-founder of Singular Law Group, argues that firms' ownership and business model goals must be more than just a different ownership structure because that is merely more of the same, just with different players. Instead, the new post-pandemic law firm should be designed around the business- and technology-savvy brought by the non-lawyers to support an approach that puts clients' needs and wants first. This chapter explores how we keep the best of the status quo while building a new firm that will absolutely delight clients in a measurable manner, to become the model for the new normal, using as a case study a brand-new law firm built entirely in the wake of the pandemic.

Many law firms underestimate the importance of commercial skills in the new normal that will develop post-pandemic. More seriously, many law firms will assume that they can build their businesses, on their own, relying on the legal talent that worked before – a decision that could lead them disastrously astray. Law firms that incorporate experience from the commercial world into driving their business forward can and will win in surprising ways. Similarly, adding non-executive voices into management teams will help firms find routes forward that avoid the pitfalls of going back to the old ways, whilst exploiting the new opportunities of the deregulated world.

In chapter seven, Jon Whittle of Jon Whittle Consulting Ltd explains why marketing and sales are going to be as important as legal talent in the post-pandemic world and why these skills need to sit as equal voices in the management of law firms. Jon also looks at the role of the consultant or independent solicitor and why this new breed of lawyer is both a threat and an opportunity to law firms going forward. Now, more than ever, being a good lawyer is definitely not enough to run a good law firm. Good law firms need, first and foremost, to be good businesses. Those that are not will struggle in the new deregulated post-pandemic world of legal services.

Many lawyers embraced remote work for meetings, trainings, and client interactions throughout 2020 and into mid-2021. Now emerging into a post-pandemic world, the question is whether our legal system, including all means of dispute resolution courts and beyond, will continue to serve people with fully remote systems. Research shows that only about three percent of all civil matters go to court, which means the "alternative" dispute resolution (ADR) avenues dominate and actually are the norm, not the exception. Within the field, there is also the early dispute resolution model, which can include training to prevent conflict or, at a minimum, plan interventions to avoid even the threat of litigation. During the pandemic, ZDR (Zoom Dispute Resolution) became the de-facto means for court, mediation, meetings, training, education, bar exams, and more. Several new technologies were launched or relaunched, including augmented or artificial intelligence (AI) for disputes. Chapter eight by Mary Juetten explores the staying power and impact of remote dispute resolution and AI on the role of lawyers and legal training.

In chapter nine, Viv Williams, consulting director of Viv Williams Consulting, explores the current legal sector, looking at the driving forces behind change. He examines the age profile of law firm owners and explores how law firm structures have changed, before reviewing the growth of Solicitor Consultant models and what impact that is having on current M&A activity.

Viv delves into the challenges brought about by succession and looks in detail at the current challenges with professional indemnity insurance and how this is the catalyst for many firms to look for mergers, the type of services currently being offered, and how technology and AI is changing their delivery, and the driving forces behind certain activities and how that will impact on smaller practices. Viv also analyses the specialist niche practice and why many firms will be forced into withdrawing services, and the numbers of law firms reducing year-on-year and how consolidation will impact the profession.

Viv predicts what the face of the legal profession will look like within the next few years, and the solutions facing numerous firms unable to find a suitable acquirer or merger partner.

The COVID-19 pandemic has had a profound impact on the global legal landscape. Unprecedented challenges, emerging risks, and shifting client priorities will fuel demand for services across many legal sectors. In chapter ten, Sally Kane and Ashley B. Jordan of Reed Smith LLP spotlight law practice areas that are flourishing in the aftermath of the pandemic as well as several trends that are reshaping the legal industry.

As lawyers emerge from the cloak of COVID-19, when their home and work lives were more inextricably linked than ever, they are seeking to incorporate the learnings of the pandemic into their new work worlds. Winning law firms will be the ones that can build in the benefits of remote and hybrid work into happier, productive, and profitable environments. This final chapter by Debbie Epstein Henry explores how a more humane approach to legal services with a heightened sensitivity to wellbeing and "welldoing" will improve connection with clients as well as the engagement of lawyers. Debbie also uncovers how to enhance not only law firm performance but also the lawyer experience to create happier, successful, and sustaining firms in the future.

About the authors

John Chisholm is a third generation "recovering" lawyer, previously a partner, managing partner, and chief executive of Australian law firms. John established his own consultancy in 2005 to share his expertise and experience with professional firms who look to maximize their performance by adopting better and different business models and mindsets. He now speaks, educates, facilitates, coaches, and consults. As a practicing lawyer, John was well placed to experience first-hand both the benefits but also the drawbacks of the professions billing their services solely by reference to time. He has worked with many professional firms (and their customers) around the world, assisting them with both a mindset change, and the practical implementation and application of moving towards a timeless pricing model. John co-founded the Innovim Group – an international advisory practice that equips knowledge firms to transform for success by helping them to understand the value they create and how to capture that value with strategic pricing. John is a senior fellow of the VeraSage Institute, an international think tank of thought leaders and innovators for professional firms, adjunct professor of Law at La Trobe University Law School (2018-2021), fellow of the College of Legal Practice Management (US) and distinguished fellow of the Centre for Legal Innovation (Aus) 2019-2020. He has written numerous articles, papers, and blogs on pricing and business model change and has presented and spoken to thousands of professionals on the topic.

Debbie Epstein Henry is an expert, bestselling author, public speaker, and podcast host on careers, workplaces, women, and law. Debbie runs DEH Consulting, Speaking, Writing and consults with and speaks at private retreats, public events, and conferences for companies, law firms, and other professional service firms as well as non-profits. Debbie's international work includes multiple engagements in The Hague as well as in Paris at the French Senate and in London and Vienna and other cities abroad. For 20 years, hundreds of news outlets have featured her work, including

The New York Times, NBC Nightly News, *The Wall Street Journal*, National Public Radio, and *The National Law Journal*. In 2020, Debbie launched a podcast, Inspiration Loves Company, where she conducts interviews and explores how to do better and be better at life, work, and everything in-between. She delves into issues including courage, women, technology, learning, race, entrepreneurship, careers, happiness, leadership, balance and more. Debbie runs the DEH Speaker Series, offering quarterly programming by webcast with *New York Times* bestselling authors, TED speakers, and thought leaders. In 2007, she conceived of the Best Law Firms for Women initiative, a national survey she developed and ran for a decade with Working Mother to annually select the top 50 law firms for women and report on industry trends. Debbie is the author of *Law and Reorder*, the #1 bestselling ABA Flagship book for 2011 and the co-author of another ABA bestselling flagship book in 2015, *Finding Bliss*. By 2008, her public speaking, press exposure and advocacy enabled her to build a national network of over 10,000 lawyers. From there, in 2011, Debbie co-founded Bliss Lawyers, a company employing high caliber attorneys to work on temporary engagements for in-house legal department and law firm clients. In 2020, Bliss Lawyers was acquired by Axiom, the global leader in high-caliber, on-demand legal talent.

Debbie volunteers her time with a number of non-profits. She is president of The Forum of Executive Women, a nomination-only, membership organization of the top 500 women in business in the Greater Philadelphia region. She also chairs Brooklyn Law School Women's Leadership Circle, which runs a national women's law student and alumnae initiative. Additionally, Debbie serves as an advisor to The Fourth Floor and an advisor to the New York State Bar Association Attorney Wellbeing Task Force.

Debbie has received numerous awards, including being named among the *Philadelphia Business Journal*'s "Women of Distinction". In 2017, Debbie received the Anne X. Alpern Award, presented annually to a female lawyer who demonstrates excellence in the legal profession and who makes a significant professional impact on women in the law. She received her BA from Yale and her JD cum laude from Brooklyn Law School.

Patricia K. Gillette is one of the country's leading experts and most sought-after speakers on gender diversity and equality. Rated as a top employment litigator and trial lawyer by *Chambers* and other organizations for 40 years and as a leader and rainmaker in her firms, Pat's legal career focused on assisting Fortune 500 companies with their most difficult issues and challenges. At the end of 2015, she resigned from her firm to pursue her passion for empowering women through keynote speaking and writing. She now tours the country speaking on issues that help women advance into leadership positions in their organizations. Pat was invited to join JAMS in 2016 and she now spends some of her time mediating employment cases.

Pat has been recognized for her work to advance women in the legal profession by many organizations. She is the 2018 recipient of the ABA Margaret Brent Award, the highest honor given to women lawyers for professional achievement and for advancing the interests of women lawyers. She has also received the ABA Golden Hammer Award, the California Women Lawyers Association's Fay Stender Award, the Transformational Leadership Award as one of the Top Women Rainmakers, and the Barristers Association of San Francisco Award of Merit.

Pat is the co-founder of the Opt-In Project, a nationwide initiative focused on changing the structure of law firms to increase the retention and advancement of women. The team she co-chaired at the 2016 Hackathon created the Mansfield Rule, which has now been adopted by several law firms and corporations across the country as a means of immediately impacting the opportunities for women to advance into leadership positions.

Pat has been a commissioner on the ABA Commission on Women in the Profession, a member of ABA's Gender Equity Task Force, co-chair of the BASF No Glass Ceiling Initiative, and has served on several non-profit boards dedicated to protecting and promoting women. She is currently a board member of DirectWomen and Girls Leadership.

Wayne Hassay began private practice in 1991 as a civil litigator and is now the managing partner of Maguire Schneider Hassay, LLP. MSH is a mid-sized law firm for the Columbus, Ohio market. He serves on the board of directors of the American Bar Association affiliated Group Legal Services Association. His law firm serves as a provider firm for the legal service plan, LegalShield. Wayne is a member of the Ohio State Bar Association's Access to Justice Task Force. He is a regional member of the Thrivent Financial Board of Directors. He is a frequent speaker and author on the evolution of the legal marketplace. As managing partner of MSH, his mission is to bring innovation and technology to the practice of law for the benefit of clients. The philosophy is to broaden access to justice by using technology in a way that helps clients afford the legal services they need. Wayne believes this will achieve the best possible result for his clients, while making their experience as stress-free as possible.

Ashley B. Jordan is a partner at Reed Smith LLP and a member of the firm's insurance recovery practice. Ashley has helped recover more than $100m in insurance proceeds for Fortune and Global 500 companies, as well as middle market businesses and individuals. She was named a 2021 "Woman of Influence: Attorneys" by the *Los Angeles Business Journal* and frequently writes and speaks on insurance coverage and risk management.

Mary Juetten, the author of *Small Law Firm KPIs: How to Measure your Way to Greater Profits* and *The Business of Legal: The Data-Driven Law Practice*, plus founder and CEO of Traklight, has dedicated her more-than-35-year career to helping businesses achieve and protect their success. Mary is a professional accountant, attorney (admitted in Arizona and Washington states), mediator and is trained in collaborative law. Specializing in leading companies in transition or start-up phases and helping them create sustainable, operational, and financial growth, Mary wants entrepreneurs and businesses to have Fortune 500 style software solutions. Using her extensive education including Bachelor of Commerce degree from McGill and a Juris Doctorate and Masters of Law from Arizona State, as well as her US and Canadian accounting and public accountant certifications, Mary created the only self-guided software platform that creates a custom intellectual property (IP) strategy plus assesses business risk.

Mary founded Juetten Law in Washington and recently Singular Law Group in Arizona and is an international author, blogger, speaker, and mentor. In 2015, Mary co-founded Evolve Law, a sales and marketing channel for Traklight, and spoke internationally on change and technology adoption in the legal industry before selling the company to Above the Law.

Mary was named to the American Bar Association's Legal Resource Technology Center 2016 Women in Legal Tech list and the FastCase Class of 2016. She also served on the Group Legal Services Association (GLSA) Board and taught both Technology Law and Access to Justice through Technology at Arizona State and lectures on the Business of Legal in Suffolk Law's legal technology program. Mary is currently on the executive committee of the alternative dispute resolution section of the Washington State Bar Association.

Sally Kane is a business development manager for Reed Smith LLP with 15 years of experience in legal marketing. A former lawyer, she has been writing on the intersection of law practice and marketing since 2005 and her work has appeared in media outlets across the globe. She previously served as editor-in-chief of a national legal magazine and as a legal careers expert for TheBalance.com.

Yvonne Nath is CEO of ALSP Advisor, a legal operations consultancy that helps law firms of all sizes create scalable business models and improve their value propositions to shareholders and clients. The lines between different types of legal service providers are blurring. Yvonne's goal is to help legal service providers of any type find their blue ocean to stand out from the competition. Yvonne is also a law firm strategy consultant with LawVision where her team has been advising law firms on strategy for more than 30 years. She has her master's degree in law firm management and is accredited in organizational culture. As a millennial, Yvonne is mindful of the impact that generational shifts, technological advances, and the evolution of work culture are having on the legal industry and she helps law firms navigate these changes. Her latest book, *The Book on Law Firm Culture*, was published in April 2021. Her thought leadership can also be found in *The American Lawyer*, Bloomberg Law, *Legaltech News*, *Legal Evolution*, *Legal Business World*, PinHawk, Law360, LawVision, Medium, Impact Lawyers, and more.

For the last ten years, **Jon Whittle** has been working with law firms developing strategies that build strong, commercially focused, businesses. Jon spent nine years in a senior leadership role at LexisNexis and is a recognized authority on what contributes to growth for law firms. Jon is a specialist in building real value using market intelligence and customer insight and is the architect and author of the widely read *LexisNexis Bellwether Reports*, which have played an important role in shaping the strategic development of law firms.

Prior to LexisNexis, Jon ran a start-up and in management consulting having previously worked for two decades in board level positions driving commercial growth for some of the world's largest intellectual property and media companies with extensive M&A experience both in the UK and internationally.

He applies the fruits of his experience to the world of law firm development and now runs his own consultancy business (Jon Whittle Consulting Ltd) whilst also working as a consultant with Viv Williams Consulting. In addition to providing consulting services directly to law firms he is a regular speaker at legal conferences and seminars and regularly writes for the legal press on the strategic future of legal markets.

Viv Williams is a leading consultant to law firms on the topics of strategy, merger and acquisition, management, practice development, and marketing. Viv's experience as a managing director of two floated plc companies adds a new dimension to law firms. He has the experience necessary to provide an invaluable practical management insight that applies to all professional firms, and is a specialist in strategy, merger and acquisition and "lean management" theory, helping law firms to evolve. He provides the vision and inspiration for law firms to become more corporate. By applying corporate governance to a modern law firm, Viv helps them to improve their management systems and increase profitability.

Viv is involved with several businesses serving the legal profession – he is the consulting director of Viv Williams Consulting, chairman of AWH Solicitors, CEO of Zaiwalla & Co and non-executive director of several law firms. Viv has written two books on law firm management and is regularly interviewed by the *Law Society Gazette* on a host of topics.

Stuart Wilson is one of a few global marketing leaders with expertise as chief marketing officer of both Big Four and Big Law professional services firms. He is an innovative and transformational C-Level marketing executive who leverages brand, business development, business intelligence, marketing communications, and digital marketing solutions to win, develop, and grow customers and clients. Throughout his career, he has advised many of the world's leading organizations regarding their marketing strategies including Coca-Cola, HSBC, InBev, P&G, American Express as well as Deloitte, PwC, EY and Lathan & Watkins. He has deep experience working across six continents and numerous geographies, having also lived and worked in London, Chicago, New York, and Toronto.

Chapter 1: COVID-19 and the rise of the 21st century law firm

By Wayne Hassay, Maguire Schneider Hassay, LLP

The words "21st century" still conjure up notions of flying cars and vacations to Mars. While we have not gotten that far, the innovations of the 21st century are vast. Seized by businesses, technology has disrupted many industries – banking, hospitality, transportation, food service, music, and communications, to name a few. These industries have all leveraged 21st century technology that consumers now expect every day.

Twenty years into the great century of technology, where does the business of law fit into the paradigm? Although there is a strong and vocal legal tech community, comparatively speaking it is very small and considered an outlier. The legal profession has remained firmly entrenched in 19th century concepts. After all, precedent rules the profession. Looking backward is the attorney's guide to the practice of law, which comes into play even as non-lawyers have employed 21st century technology to erode the purview of lawyers.

The precedential status quo had long been self-evidently broken. For example, for a multitude of reasons, the status quo has denied access to justice for your typical consumer. Even a resulting wage decrease for small and solo lawyers did not stymie the long-term malaise. Then an acute disease struck the legal profession – the COVID-19 pandemic. In the COVID age, partners were missing draws, associates and partners alike were dismissed. This was serious. As the pandemic raged, many law firms were forced, perhaps for the first time ever, to reconsider how business was done. Necessity became the mother of innovation.

Pre-pandemic, the legal profession had long been stalled at the crossroads of tradition and innovation. It is disconcerting that in a profession sworn to protect the public, it took self-interest and survival to spawn innovation, which in turn helps consumers and improves the profession for lawyers and staff alike. Despite this flurry of innovation that the pandemic brought to so many law firms and lawyer practices alike, the fact that some competitors have made such changes is likely unbeknownst to those who merely hunkered down to weather the COVID storm. The pandemic caused some lawyers to make massive changes for the inner workings of the law firm – flexible work schedules, fully-remote offices, revised resource allocations, embracing new client expectations, and even casual wear while working. For those that did not just hunker down, are these pandemic-propelled innovations permanent?

The seeds of innovation

Although uncertain how this should be characterized – some lawyers may say thankfully, luckily, or coincidently, while others may say unfortunately – the seeds of innovation existed long before the pandemic. Considering a profession stuck in a 19th century mindset, this feels shockingly unexpected.

For instance, the profession must be eternally grateful to those fringe legal technologists. As noted, effecting change in the legal profession is a steep slope. Keep in mind lawyers who first used email or the cloud were at times threatened with disbarment under the guise of confidentiality or other silly arguments. More likely the real reason was lawyers who understood nothing about technology merely sensed a threat from innovative lawyers who might disrupt the tried-and-true money-making models of the traditional law firms. It is hard to believe something as ubiquitous as email and the cloud were forced into the profession by innovators years ago and ultimately helped maintain it during the pandemic. This should be an important lesson.

More surprisingly, should the traditional law firm thank the business models operated by non-lawyers, which have long sought to disrupt the legal marketplace? There is much to learn from these organizations, i.e., online legal form providers, lead generators, legal service plans, and alternative legal service providers. Undoubtedly, pre-pandemic, the prevailing perception was these organizations sought only to erode lawyer purview. And – let this record reflect – a few of these organizations may still erode fundamental values that protect consumers. Regardless, before the pandemic, prospective clients were often hard to reach because of solicitation rules. In the height of pandemic lockdowns, prospective clients were even harder to reach. Meanwhile, these organizations with alternative business models were firmly entrenched where the clients could be safely found amid a pandemic – on the internet. Existing and implemented technology allowed these organizations to create remote communication avenues with prospective clients and provide access to justice, making them better poised to address the pandemic than the traditional legal profession.

Some Bar Associations must also be given credit for sowing the seeds of innovation. Select Bar Associations led the progressive charge while others filed failed lawsuits against alternative legal service providers. The more forward-thinking Bars issued futures reports and have task forces designed to increase access to justice in this age of technology. These Bars try to move their membership, but movement is difficult as the rank-and-file are generally bogged down in the daily practice of law.

Meanwhile, professional responsibility authorities have recently revised rules with a specific goal of modernization. Little did they know those changes likely improved or even saved some law careers amid the pandemic. Consider these recent amendments in some jurisdictions regarding:

- Virtual law offices;
- Multiple jurisdictional law practice;
- Limited scope services;
- Revised solicitation rules; and
- Non-lawyer ownership of law firms.

While each carry with it debate and controversy, especially non-lawyer law firm ownership, without these rule revisions innovation may have been curtailed during the crisis. Granted, innovation would still have occurred outside of the rules out of necessity and survival. But for a profession obsessed with the past, the timing of these revisions was fortuitous.

And then there was a pandemic...

Leading up to the first quarter of 2020, everything was steaming along fine for solo, small, and mid-sized law firms, right? Sure, practicing law was a daily grind. The hours necessary to find and service clients seemed to be getting longer and longer. Hourly rates may have increased, but did the delivery of the service change or improve? Even when clients were found, it seemed fewer and fewer could afford to pay. Who was really getting ahead? Regardless, this daily hustle was the status quo. Not great but still a living and occasionally rewarding work. What could go wrong?

Then came the pandemic, and the traditional law office model was quickly placed in a precarious position. Could lawyers even report to the office? Lockdown orders referred to essential services. Sure, legal services are essential but not like the delivery of gasoline, police protection, or baby formula, especially when courts are closed. In the first weeks in many jurisdictions, lawyers were not even deemed essential. Perhaps that was an oversight, but it served as a wake-up call. Who could pay rent, employee salaries, and tuition for the kids if the job was at a complete standstill? While there are pockets of tremendous success among lawyers, en masse lawyers run small businesses not unlike the café down the street. Our vaunted legal system screeched to a halt. Granted, some courts quickly reopened but often only partially. What good are courts with a moratorium on civil dockets? With many legal deadlines stayed, the system that drives clients to finally take advice, close cases, and hence pay lawyers, crashed. Well over a year later, some courts have yet to fully reopen civil dockets. The legal profession has always felt immune from the ups and downs of the economy. In fact, historically difficult economic times often spawned business for lawyers. But this time was different. Even the lifeblood of law practice – servicing clients face-to-face – came to a halt.

Things were not great before and now things became a little worse. There was nothing anyone could do, right? Many, not just lawyers, merely hoped for a rapidly developing "new normal", which was just code for the status quo plus mask wearing, hand washing, and social distancing. The seeds of innovation, however, were there. Some seized and are continuing to seize opportunities.

The rise of the pandemic-era law firm

What did the enterprising or desperate lawyer do? In lockdown they had some free time from the rat race of practicing law. So, some experimented.

Law firms had always planned to stay in touch but how many really did? Amid the pandemic, consumers were desperate for information they could trust. If only a law firm had a way to reach those consumers and in a socially distant manner. For those firms who had the seeds of innovation, for example mass emails, social media, video conferencing and live internet events, it was easy. Perhaps once considered fringe marketing efforts for a busy lawyer, these methods became a communication lifeline between lawyer and consumer. Those who employed these methods first developed trust, relationships, and convenience with consumers in the crisis. A priceless connection amid lockdowns and for the future.

Then there was the desperate search for new clients. Lawyers could no longer randomly search for clients at in-person political or community events. One-at-a-time client acquisition had been the bulwark of legal practice. Pause and think about this ridiculous business model in the modern world. Many lawyers had been raised to believe advertising was unprofessional and even a threat to their license on the whim of an interpretation of vague terms in professional responsibility rules. Necessity, however, required better websites and an explosion of social media of all kinds. Whatever could be done quickly, inexpensively, and could reach clients became much more mainstream. It is also safe to conclude more lawyers became amenable to those non-lawyer alternative legal service organizations that were willing to work with them. Lawyers often had to do so amid murky 20th century professional responsibility rules. Here again, necessity is the mother of innovation.

When a client was found in the pandemic era, what happened next? Was an in-person meeting even permitted? If yes, what client wanted to risk a plague to see a lawyer? Certainly, lawyers were perplexed. Historically, there was only one way to see a client and that was in-person and in the office. Seemingly making a client drive to the office, often pay to park, and wait 45 minutes in the lobby was part of the overall aesthetic of hiring a lawyer. Before the pandemic, proper procedure required that a lawyer sign-up a client by making notes on a legal pad during an in-person conference while on the clock. This lawyer-centric perspective came to a screeching halt in the pandemic. Post-pandemic, consumers will not return to a less advantageous way of life. Consumers will gravitate to lawyers that offer remote meetings, robust and convenient communication by email, text, recorded or live video, electronic signatures and notarizations, lower-cost, limited-scope services, and full-service client-facing portals.

As workloads shrunk, certainly there was a sense more work had to be found. Much had been written about an untapped market of consumer legal needs. The pandemic brought to the forefront the hope that work could be generated in high volume, remotely, and driven by technology. This is in fact one definition of limited scope services. In the bespoke world of legal services this was long ignored. Lowering the cost per unit while increasing the revenue on volume – in other words, scaling – had simply been exotic thinking. Despite limited scope rules being on the books for years, the consternation was, what if a judge did not permit a lawyer to withdraw from a case? Supposedly the innovation was deemed too risky by most because of this one occasional possibility of a dimwitted judge being unable to understand a rule. More likely the motive was, if full freight hourly work was still the norm (even if accounts receivable mounted) why charge less money for limited scope work; what if the volume never materialized? It is sad to again ponder that it took a pandemic to broaden access to justice. It is safe to conclude, however, that the pandemic led to inquiries into document automation, artificial intelligence and the alike became more mainstream efforts.

Workloads slowed but work still needed to be done. Employees may have been forbidden to report to the office or at least some were uncomfortable with doing so. Nor could a law firm risk its workforce getting sick. It was imperative to implement the firm's disaster recovery plan. Before the pandemic, disaster recovery plans were likely the folly of a law firm's IT specialist, if indeed the firm even had an IT specialist. Amid lockdowns, imagine the shock when many lawyers discovered their phone system was not in the cloud and therefore employees could not access client calls from home. Of course, the same realization applied to accounting, document, and word processing systems. If there was no disaster recovery plan, lawyers quickly created one so that employees could work remotely. Literally overnight, thousands of virtual law offices were created by law firms that would have never dreamed of such.

Some, for one reason or another, did not implement a remote workplace. Some desired it but could not because they could not get the technology in place. On the other end of the spectrum, some lawyers did not perceive a disaster and insisted on running their businesses as near the old status quo as possible. One's perspective regarding the pervasiveness of the pandemic is not germane to this chapter. However, it is undeniable the pandemic taught many lawyers they could run their law firms remotely, at a much lower cost and therefore higher profitability. It says much about the legal profession and its relationship to tradition, that as retail and commercial office space rapidly evolves, many lawyers believe virtual legal work remains impossible. Granted, virtual or mostly virtual law firms have new organizational, ethical, and managerial challenges. It should go without saying, increased profit will carry the day. Furthermore, clients will also perpetuate innovation. Legal fees may no longer need to subsidize expensive real estate and clients crave convenience. Overall, those who got a leg up with virtual work during the pandemic have a strategic advantage.

Let us not forget how employees play into this equation. To be frank, partners want profit. Consumers want the aforementioned conveniences and, even if they do not fully understand it, need zealous advocacy by lawyers. What makes all of this come together? Employees.

The historical law firm was based on the concept of presenteeism for administrative employees and lawyer employees alike. One had to be present at the office eight or more hours a day or the contribution was unacceptable. This even required fashionable dress and generally a walk by the managing partner's office to prove attendance. A soul-crushing routine for any self-respecting professional. The routine remained despite being long ago made obsolete by modern communication and software that accurately measures contribution.

The pandemic has annihilated law office presenteeism. Law firms that seized the uninvited opportunities of the pandemic have learned presenteeism is not the driver of success. In fact, presenteeism dampens morale. The pandemic-era law firm realized quality employees will have a choice of how, where, and when they work. The best employees are not going back to a less advantageous way of life. They will merely seek and find law firms that offer innovative solutions. A new focus must be on efficiency, teamwork, culture, and camaraderie, as opposed to always but merely being present.

The rise of the 21st century law firm

The pandemic shook all marketplaces, including law. Halting innovation was impossible while weathering the pandemic. Now as the dust settles, will the profession try to stem the tide of innovation? Consider perhaps a few small law firms shrunk or even closed their doors because they could not stay competitive. Thus, in the eyes of some, the pandemic may have culled the herd a bit and that is OK because it merely means more business for those who stayed in business. Therefore, some may consider COVID-19 a blip that effected just a few quarters of business. Now the respected profession of law must wish to get back to business as usual, the pre-pandemic normal.

The profession would be naïve to believe it can turn back the effects of the cataclysmic pandemic. Some lawyers will be more aggressively innovative than ever before. They will beat the competition, make more money, and marginalize those who watch from the sidelines. If not lawyers, then non-lawyers will engage the consumers.

The guiding light must be the consumers themselves. Historically, consumers have been viewed as rarely needing but not generally wanting legal services. But this perception is a function of the access they had to legal services. Post-pandemic, consumers will demand and receive more than ever ease of use and communication, including free market and truthful solicitation, self-help, transparency, greater affordability, efficiency, mobility, and top-notch advocacy and independent professional judgment when necessary. The innovative path focuses on the wants and needs of the consumer and not the preconceived notion of how the business of law has been done. In other words, just as every other free market industry works – lawyers, welcome to the 21st century.

Chapter 2: Pricing and business model change post-COVID-19

By John Chisholm, John Chisholm Consulting

Some perspective

There has been, and will continue to be, much written and spoken about the effect the COVID-19 pandemic has had on our personal lives, on our families, our communities, our nations, our economies, and on businesses. The legal profession is not immune from any of this of course. Nearly every aspect of the legal profession – from private law firms, the judiciary, to the law guilds themselves – have shouted from the rooftops about how the profession has adapted to the "challenge" of COVID-19, by adopting different practices including working from home, increasing the use of technology, virtual online attendances, and more humanistic policies, to name but a few – as though any of these were exclusive to the legal profession.[1] They are not.

The legal profession generally and this chapter specifically needs to be considered in the wider context of COVID-19. What happens in the legal profession is usually not per se a life and death issue. However, I believe – and I hope this chapter will convince you likewise – that if the legal profession could make a paradigm shift and adopt a sustainably different mindset and business model, among many other benefits will be substantial improvement to the wellness and wellbeing of those who work with and within our profession.

Pricing

If any business owner disputes that pricing has by far the greatest impact on the profitability of any business, they should not be in business. Law firms are a business. It therefore seems odd to me that now in the third decade of the 21st century, the legal profession – and regrettably still only a minority of the profession – is only just starting to talk about *prices*. This is notwithstanding that many BigLaw firms now employ professionals that have the word "pricing" somewhere in their title and/or are – at face value anyway – responsible for their firm's pricing, and/or engage external pricing consultants to assist with their firm's pricing.

Lawyers love precedents and conventions so it is perhaps not surprising that the habits and learnings of two or three generations of lawyers are hard to change – especially if those habits are considered to have been financially successful for lawyers. My observations anecdotally are that the rank and file of the vast majority of law firm owners and partners still talk in terms of *hourly rates* – not prices. This is of course perpetuated by the processes, measurements, incentives, and rewards in those firms being principally – if not solely – built around hourly rates and time.

The "OldLaw" business and "pricing" model

As a former practicing lawyer, I realize definitions are important – especially to other lawyers – so let us first define what a business model is, secondly what a traditional law firm business model looks like, and thirdly what defines pricing.

There are many variations on the definition of a business model in any organization but the one I am attracted to is the simplicity largely based on the works of Alexander Osterwalder:[2]

> *"How does your firm/company create value for and capture a portion of that value from its customers?"*

The business model most law firms in the western world have utilized since the second half of the 20th century – what I term the "OldLaw" business model – essentially leverages people x time x hourly rate. It needs little explanation.

At its most simplistic level, *pricing* is the monetary compensation someone is willing to pay for a good or service. In the business world, price(s) are normally agreed up front before or at the time of making a purchase. Price is not only one of the 4Ps of marketing,[3] but is intrinsically linked to the value (perceived or otherwise) of any purchase.

In the law firm context, for the last 15 years or so I, along with many others including my colleagues from The VeraSage Institute,[4] have been imploring professionals – especially lawyers – to transform their business model and not only ditch the billable hour but also to burn their timesheets.

I didn't always hold this view. I remember time before the billable hour. As a young partner in an Australian law firm in the early 1980s, I was swayed to introduce timesheets and time-based billing into our firm, not because clients demanded them, but because other law firms were doing it and we wanted to copy and look the same as them.

As a partner, managing partner and CEO of two reasonably large Australian law firms for over 20 years, I have never suggested billing by time didn't have its advantages for law firms. It was (and is) largely profitable – but it is a lazy billing model. It was never a pricing model. *Pricing* is what you do up front before the work has commenced. *Billing* is what you do after the work is done. *Pricing* is prospective – billing, and especially billing by time, is retrospective. Pricing is accurate and transparent. *Billing* by time is inaccurate and non-transparent.[5]

Provided law firms adhered to a leverage model and could increase their hourly rates year on year higher than what their costs (which are predominantly fixed) were likely to be, and clients were prepared to pay those hourly rates and the time spent, it wasn't all that difficult to be profitable.

It was also an easy pitch to clients too – *"You only pay for our time spent, nothing more – and we will show you our time sheets too."*

But as we know, it also caused some problems with clients. Lack of certainty and predictability around fees and the inevitable *bill shock* was a source of irritation to clients (and continues to be) often resulting in trust with clients taking a hit – not to mention firm "write offs". Revenue, realization rates, and utilization became OldLaw's internal talisman.

There were some downsides for firms as well. It didn't take long for the model to foster a production mentality in many firms. It meant the slowest horse could often win the race and sometimes good, experienced lawyers might be financially penalized if they could get a job done quicker than a competitor – or even a colleague! This may seem counterintuitive but over the years I have seen many pricing mistakes by good lawyers and firms and most of those pricing mistakes resulted in those firms undervaluing their services and leaving value on the table.

As time billing pressures increased over time (excuse the pun) this caused increasing dissatisfaction, stress-related and wellness issues for some lawyers, many of whom left the private profession to get away from the seemingly relentless pressure and the deleterious effects of time-based billing and filling out time sheets in six-minute increments. No one went to law school to learn to be the best time recorder. As a profession we claim we recruit the best, the brightest, the most creative – and then make them account for every six minutes of their day?

As the late Dr Michael Hammer[6] once said:

"A professional is someone who is responsible for achieving a result rather than performing a task."

One of the major problems with the billable hour model is that it focuses lawyers on tasks, activities, and inputs instead of what really matters to clients – *outputs, outcomes, and results.*

Maybe not really fee pressures but predictability pressures?

For some years now we have all read the pleas from clients of big-end-of-town firms – lawyers themselves – who allegedly want "more for less". No surprises here. We all want more for less if we can – without of course compromising on quality. We would also hear snippets from some in-house counsel complaining about the billable hour model.

I happen to think, especially at the big end of town, that the call from many in-house purchasers of legal services was as much, if not more, about obtaining more predictability and certainty around legal spend rather than simply sourcing cheaper legal fees or even moving away from the billable hour model. After all, most GCs came from OldLaw and were brought up on the billable hour model. To the credit of the profession, even if their core business model remained the same, more and more firms under pressure from some clients began experimenting with and offering different billing and pricing models. Very few big-end-of-town firms now only offer hourly rates. The most common alternatives became fixed fees, capped, or blended hourly rates. The latter two models are totally related to time and are retrospective and even fixed fees or menu pricing themselves are also often linked to anticipated time in advance.[7]

Meanwhile, at the other end – the consumer end – access to justice and to legal services remains an increasing problem and "the gap" it seems is ever widening. Many law firms have left the consumer market or been driven out of it in droves as most cannot make a profit, while consumers themselves have turned increasingly to *alternative* business model providers, and online offerings such as LegalZoom[8] and others.

Did the business model change during COVID-19?

Although I am fortunate to work with many lawyers and other professionals around the world who have or are changing their business model, and in particular moving away from the billable hour and timesheets, to date these tend to be mainly boutique specialist firms which are run by leaders who are genuinely innovative, risk averse, want to be different to their competitors, make a positive improvement to their culture and team, and have deeper and more meaningful client relationships. The professionals who run such firms in the main were doing this irrespective of COVID-19, although from my experience and observation the increase in interest and demand for different business and pricing models has definitely increased during the pandemic. These firms have burned their timesheets, adopted value-based pricing, and/or in increasing numbers, moved to subscription models.

For the majority of firms at the big end of town though, the answer is "no" – their business model per se has not changed even if more and more of these firms have employed pricing professionals and in some areas of their practices are genuinely using upfront pricing, quotations, more accurate estimates, fixed fees, and for others even success fees, contingency fees, phased or milestone fees and the like. To be fair some are even running pilot programs with clients experimenting with aspects of value-based pricing and more elaborate retainer and subscription models.

Those firms, however, still require their professionals to fill out timesheets, measure and reward themselves and their professionals by time, and as such will always – even with the best will in the world – continue to default to time. Time recording in a professional firm is a huge innovation and collaboration killer and, in my view, severely limits a firm's real potential.[9]

Obtaining reliable and accurate statistics from the legal profession on the use and success of genuine up front pricing models is notoriously difficult and even though the billable hour model still remains the norm at present, there is little doubt that other fee models are gaining in use and popularity year-on-year.

The post-COVID law firm: timeless

There is now irrefutable evidence that law firms can ditch timesheets and the billable hour and still be viable and profitable. Moreover, the ones that have taken that step report the following benefits:

- Substantially improved profit and cashflow;
- Reduction and often complete elimination of cost disputes with clients;
- Improved value creation for clients;
- Enhanced relationships of trust with clients; and
- A genuinely much more inclusive and collaborative internal culture.

While the balance of this chapter mainly deals with lawyers moving to a value-based pricing model, I am a huge advocate of the adoption of both value-based pricing and subscription-based models in law firms. Subscription models are the fastest growing business model in the world now and they are increasingly being used in the law world, not just by online providers such as LegalZoom but also more and more hitherto traditional firms. Subscription models might also not just be the savior of some firms but the savior of the legal profession, longer term.[10]

Both models are *timeless*, require firms to price their services up-front based on the perceived value they are going to provide to their clients, and to implement successfully lawyers first need to have a value conversation with their client to understand what is important to them, what they value, what they want, and importantly what they need.

There are, however, important differences and considerations required for firms that wish to adopt a subscription model, which this chapter will not delve into except to point out that a value-based model in the main still prices *transactions* with your client, whereas a subscription model prices the *relationship* with your client.

In a value-based environment, firms need to scope the value and the work and, after agreeing on the scope, agree on the price(s). As mentioned previously, the price is based on outcomes, results, and outputs, all of which are important to clients, not retrospective fees based on inputs and activities or firms' own costs, none of which are important to clients. If the scope changes, so might the price but you will always agree change of scope and change of price up-front.

Incentives matter

The four prime reasons given by for the retention of timesheets are:

1. We need them for pricing;
2. We need them for project management;
3. We need them to evaluate the efficiency of our lawyers; and
4. We need them for cost accounting – assessing profitability per client, or per matter.

Each one of these justifications have been debunked over and over again.[11] But for firms that have transitioned to or started up a new practice where there are no billable hours and no tracking of time, how do they measure a lawyer's productivity, worth, and contribution to the firm? In most timeless firms, hourly billing and timesheets are replaced by:

- Price-led costing;
- A value council, a chief value officer, and/or a firm-wide policy of no one pricing their own work;

- Fixed price agreements, variation requests, and offering a number of options (when you offer options, your clients will more likely consider *how* they will work with you rather than *whether* they will work with you);
- Better project management;
- Capacity and cash flow modelling;
- Key Predictive Indicators – firm-wide and individual (mentioned below); and
- After-action reviews.

Some firm-wide Key Predictive Indicators

At the VeraSage Institute we use the term *Key Predictive Indicators* as distinct from *Key Performance Indicators*, because they are much more predictive of any firm's future and ongoing success compared to traditional KPIs, which in the main are lagging indicators.

Below are examples of four firm-wide Key Predictive Indicators used by some firms that have quit using timesheets for a more client-focused set of predictive indicators.

1. Turnaround time (file velocity)

The only time clients should really be concerned about is turnaround or elapsed time. *"When am I going to get the advice, solution, guidance promised?"* So, it makes sense for firms to track at both a firm-wide and individual level when each matter comes in, establishing a desired completion date and measuring the percentage of on-time delivery.

2. Value gap

This measurement attempts to expose any gap between how much a firm could be yielding from its clients compared to how much it actually is. An excellent way to reward cross-selling additional services, increase the lifetime value of the firm to the client, and gain a larger percentage of a client's work.

3. Innovation revenue

Most law firms spout innovation as a key core of their practice, yet how many firms actually measure, track, and reward innovation? For example, what percentage of your revenue now comes from services you didn't offer three years ago?

4. Client loyalty and referrals

Referrals from existing clients are a leading indicator that the firm is delighting its current clients. It makes no sense to take on new clients if existing clients are not happy; therefore, firms need to track their current clients' above-average satisfaction and happiness (stickiness).

Individual Key Predictive Indicators

While the firm-wide Key Predictive Indicators can also be used for individuals, many firms have adopted additional ones for individuals. The better firms refrain from taking a cookie cutter approach. Every professional has their own strengths and weaknesses, which add their own imprint to any firm's success. They long ago worked out that one size does not fit all.

Individual Key Performance Indicators I have seen used by some timeless firms include such things as:

- Client feedback;
- Effective listening and communication skills;
- Risk taking, innovation, and creativity;
- Effective delegation;
- Ability to deal with change, adaptability;
- Continuous learning and mentoring;
- Personal development or marketing plans;
- Financial health, including pricing, billing practices, and recovery; and
- Client contacts per week.

Some practical tips if you really want to move to a post-COVID timeless model

Every professional and firm that I know of that has made or is making the transition away from billing by time to pricing by value has done it differently to suit their particular practice, their people, and their clients. What works for one firm will not necessarily work for another. While these are my top tips and traps based on my own experiences, from what I have seen works and doesn't work, at the end of the day firms will need to experiment, test, and adopt a trial-and-error approach to ultimately work out what best suits their practice and their clients.[12]

1. Read, read, and read some more… and then talk to someone

You are not the first nor will you be the last law firm to make the transition to a timeless pricing model so make the most of those that have gone before you. There is a wealth of material from books, blogs, articles, websites, and podcasts out there. After some reading, speak to some who have done it. I have found that most professionals who have made the move are more than happy to share their experiences.

2. Communicate, communicate, communicate

All stakeholders should know what you are doing and why you are doing it. After all, you will need all the help you can get. Everyone has a role to play in an effective transition. Meet with your team, discuss the pros and cons of the move, what affect it might have on your practice, on which clients, where is the low hanging fruit both internally and externally, where your pockets of most resistance are likely to come from, and so on. Persuading your clients about "what's in it for them" to move away from billing in arrears to pricing up front will be so much easier once you and your team know why you are making the transition. Collaboration, both internally and externally, is key to both initial implementation and ongoing success.

3. To price properly for value, you should stop recording time

I do understand how difficult it is for many lawyers to stop recording time, and many firms have successfully introduced value-based pricing model whilst maintaining timesheets – for a period. All I can tell you, overwhelmingly, is those firms that ultimately made the transition to value pricing say, if they had their time again, they would have stopped recording time sooner. No matter how hard one tries, timesheets keep you mired in time. Sooner or later, you have to break the link between time and value, and I would implore you to do it sooner.

4. Understand value-based pricing is a business model change – not a billing model change

If moving away from billing by time was just a billing model change, it might be relatively easy. It is not. It is not just about moving away from time-based billing. Discovering or adhering to your firm's purpose, fostering a culture of innovation, better and more focused client selection, better project management, using leading indicators predictive of performance, and eradication of annual performance appraisals all go hand in hand with a timesheet-free environment. All of this will be more attractive to both your lawyers of the future and the type of clients you want to attract to the firm.

5. Have a value conversation with every client and price your client, not the work

You can't talk about scope – let alone price – until you understand what your client needs. To do this, you need to have a conversation with your client about what they value. Value is subjective. Each client will have their own different perception of value. Unless your client understands the value that you are proposing to create, there is a good chance the price you quote will be too high. If you don't understand the value that you create, there is a risk that the price you quote will be too low. If it is too high, you risk the quote not being accepted. If it is too low, you risk leaving value on the table. In theory, you may have different prices for the same work to be undertaken for two different clients. The reality is that no two matters are exactly the same. Remember, just as all value is subjective, so all prices are contextual.

6. Don't price your own work

There is a reason authors and actors have agents. It is difficult to be objective about the value you are creating for your client in the work that you will do. I will be bold as lions pricing your work. Why? Because I do not have to face your client. That is why I have often found partners are the worst pricers. Most larger practices have a pricing professional or something akin to a pricing or a value council, and smaller practices might involve their support people in pricing considerations. Many firms simply have a policy that no one prices their own work and always use a buddy for pricing. The buddy shouldn't always be the same person. Spread it around to get some perspective.

7. Get better at saying "no"

You cannot value-price the wrong client. To price for value, you need to retain your self-esteem, and have a bit of an ego. You also have to be prepared to walk away. Baker's Law – *"Bad clients drive out good clients"* – suggests the price isn't wrong. The client is. Being prepared to say "no" to a client is so powerful in transforming your practice. There is great nobility in being paid what you are worth.

8. Make the complex simple and the simple compelling

Sometimes lawyers do the very opposite – we are often perceived by our clients as making a mountain out of a mole hill or trying to find problems that aren't there. Add this to the time-based billing model and we can appreciate why clients sometimes get the feeling we place our own interests ahead of our clients. My advice, especially in the beginning of your move away from time-based pricing, is not to make it too complex. For instance, if you are really struggling to price the whole transaction, price it in stages. While we may agonize over price, in the main clients tend not to. You won't always get the price right – no one does – and there is no "perfect price". As long as you learn from both your pricing failures and your pricing successes, you and your team will become more confident and more competent in pricing. If your client does not understand the value you are providing, it is not your client's mistake, it is yours.

9. Understand and practice the "five Cs of value"

For any lawyer to price on purpose you must understand the five Cs of value, which are:

- Comprehend the value we are providing to our clients;
- Create value for clients;
- Communicate the value we create;
- Convince clients they must pay for value; and
- Capture value with strategic pricing based on value, not on our costs and efforts.

10. Provide a service guarantee

The best vendors with the best products or services always guarantee them but this is something that strikes fear into the hearts of most lawyers. But you already do it without expressing it. You are guaranteeing the service the client is signing up for, not the outcome. A service that is guaranteed is worth more than a service that is not. It empowers clients. Few clients will ever call on a service guarantee. If they do, you will feel good about having the discussion. How can there be a costs dispute if you have given a service guarantee?

Final comment

If the legal profession continues to measure and reward time, that is what we will get – and we will get it in spadefuls! As Matthew Burgess, ex BigLaw partner and now owner of specialist estate planning firm View Legal,[13] which long ago adopted a value-based pricing and subscription model, says, "*With timesheets you think what is billable. Without timesheets you think what is valuable.*"

Wouldn't you, your team, and your clients agree that thinking *what is valuable* as distinct from *what is billable* is a much better way to practice your craft?

References

1. It is worth remembering that while to the legal profession's credit, it did adopt different practices and processes to meet and comply with the COVID-19 pandemic, pre-COVID many of these new and in most cases better practices were deemed impossible to implement, especially in private law firms. For example, if you asked most law firm leaders pre-COVID whether their people could work from home or whether you could successfully communicate with clients, colleagues, and the judicial system remotely, the answers would have been "no". Whether such practices are sustainable and become the post-COVID "norm" are outside the ambit of this chapter.
2. Alexander Osterwalder is a Swiss business theorist, author, and entrepreneur. Notably he was the inventor of the Business Model Canvas and co-founder of Strategyzer: http://alexosterwalder.com
3. The other three "Ps" of marketing are of course Product, Place, and Promotion.
4. Co-founded by Ron Baker, the world's leading authority in pricing in professional firms, in 2001 The VeraSage Institute espouses revolutionary thinking for professionals as well as being on a quest to rid the billable hour from professional knowledge firms: www.verasage.com. I have been a senior fellow of The VeraSage Institute since 2011. Ron Baker's seminal book, *Implementing Value Pricing: A radical business model for professional firms* (2010, Wiley Professional Advisory Services) is the lead authority in this area.
5. See my 2018 article, "Time Billing Is Accurate, Transparent and Ethical": www.chisconsult.com/my-perspective/2018/august/time-billing-furphies
6. Dr Michael Hammer, *Beyond Reengineering: How the Process-Centered Organization is Changing Our Work and Our Lives*. Harper Business, 1997: see also www.hammerandco.com
7. For a summary of the differences between value-based pricing, fixed fees, and menu prices, see: www.innovim.com.au/innovim-insights/fixed-menu-and-value-based-pricing
8. LegalZoom's recent IPO values the online legal platform in excess of US$7bn: www.cnbc.com/2021/06/30/legalzoom-debuted-up-30percent-ceo-sells-further-push-into-digital-market.html
9. See "Why time recording limits your firm's potential": www.chisconsult.com/my-perspective/2021/january/time-recording-limitations
10. For a quick but very informative look as to how subscription models can and are being used in law firms, see New Zealand legal consultant Simon Tupman's interview with Ron Baker: www.simontupman.com/law-chat. For more of a deep

dive into subscription-based models, read Mark Stiving's latest book, *Win, Keep, Grow*: https://impactpricing.com/resources/books/

11. See for example this article in *Firm of the Future* by Ron Baker: www.firmofthefuture.com/content/why-timesheets-focus-firm-leaders-on-the-wrong-things
12. I am often asked when is the right time to change your business model? Maybe the answer lies here: www.innovim.com.au/innovim-insights/blog-post-title-one-82g24
13. https://viewlegal.com.au

Chapter 3:

Never let a good crisis go to waste – creating value from the COVID-19 experience

By Stuart Wilson, chief executive officer, BIRA

In the waning months of the devastating Second World War, with the world's leaders looking toward a post-war future, Winston Churchill, amongst others, called upon these leaders to create the UN. His call to action was characterized by another of his famous quotes, "*Never let a good crisis go to waste*". The recognition that in the wake of a terrible war there was an opportunity to embrace change in a manner that was previously unachievable resulted in one of the longest periods of global peace and prosperity.

COVID-19, the first global pandemic in more than 100 years, created international economic devastation and human misery not seen since the Second World War. But similarly to the opportunity identified by Churchill, global leaders, including law firm leaders, have an opportunity to harness many of the changes forced upon them to create a new positive future.

COVID-19 change

There has been much debate about when and how COVID-19 began, but for most law firms the period immediately following the 11 March 2020 declaration of COVID-19 as a global pandemic was the defining point. In the weeks immediately following this announcement, approximately 80 percent of law firms transitioned to some form of remote working, with 50 percent doing it almost instantaneously.[1]

At the same time, in house counsel put on hold their business as usual work and instead focused on immediate pandemic response work. These law firm clients grappled with the implications of the pandemic on everything from health and safety, employment rights, and remote working scenarios to redundancies and customer liability.

In the remainder of Q2 2020, law firms took fast and dramatic action to respond to the crisis. In addition to moving to a remote working model, 46 percent reduced partner draws, 40 percent reduced fee earner salaries, 32 percent reduced staff salaries and 36 percent laid off staff. [2]

Over the subsequent months, many law firms continued to focus on what they could do to reduce their overall cost structures. Amongst the most notable areas for cost reductions were office services (22.5 percent), recruiting (40 percent), PD (42 percent) and marketing (44 percent).[3]

As a result of this unprecedented action, the COVID-19 crisis has, according to Peer Monitor Economic Index,[4] been one of the most positive economic periods for law firms since 2006. Far from being a crisis, the pandemic has in fact been a boon.

But the question now, as we hopefully look toward the end of the full-scale COVID-19 crisis, is where do law firms and their leadership go from here?

What's next? Seven strategies for the post COVID-19 law firm

As early as the summer of 2020, people were writing about "How to survive in the post-COVID-19 world".[5] These early prognostications were linked to the collective optimism that COVID-19 would be over as quickly as it started, and that as soon as the warm weather came it would miraculously disappear.[6]

The reality has been far from anything close. The numerous false dawns, along with new COVID-19 variants and mixed results in the vaccine roll out, have all contributed to a much longer than expected period of shut down, limitations on travel, and continued economic dislocation. But, at risk of falling into the same trap, the 2022 law firm business planning cycle, which often starts in September, is an appropriate time for law firms to plan their post COVID-19 future. If they aren't already doing so, this is the opportunity to leverage the gains made during the pandemic and strategize for the post-pandemic world.

As part of this strategic review it is important that leaders look toward these seven strategies for success.

1. Re-envision the future of the law firm.
2. Focus on strategic planning, not just financial planning.
3. Harness new-found partner cohesion to drive further change and deliver better results.
4. Double down on technology solutions to deliver efficiency and growth.
5. Capture savings and invest in areas that made sense to cut, but now make sense to grow.
6. Identify and invest in future areas of business growth.
7. Harness new ways of working to build teams, motivate staff, and build a stronger firm for the future.

1. Re-envision the future of the law firm

We're all very familiar with the refrain that law firms are in a negative spiral of declining fees, realization, and revenues. This is juxtaposed against an increasingly demanding procurement-led client that's turning to alternate legal service providers and innovative technology solutions to secure better service at lower cost. Add to this a much overdue investment in people, technology, and organizational infrastructure and law firms face a perfect storm.

But hold on! Haven't law firms, according to Peer Monitor Economic Index,[7] had their best financial results in close to 15 years? While true, it would be difficult to suggest that the past 18 months are a solid predictor of the future 18 months and beyond.

That said, one of the most important learnings and potentially most decisive developments for law firms over the past 15 years has been how quickly law firm leaders were able to make tough decisions to not only survive but thrive during the COVID-19 crisis.

I have written on a number of occasions about how difficult it is for law firms to re-envision their strategy and implement a new one. But COVID-19 changed something for law firms. They went from a seemingly interminable inability for their partners to make the tough decisions to making these decisions in a blink of an eye.

As the *2020 Bloomberg Law Firm Benchmark Survey* noted, within weeks of the COVID-19 outbreak being characterized as a pandemic, more than 50 percent of law firms had employees working from home. Ultimately that number would be 75 percent, with 20 percent of firms having all of their employees working from home. While certainly in line with a broader market trend, this was radical and unprecedented action by law firms, action that would have been unthinkable prior to the crisis.

The question now for law firms is how they take this recent example of their willingness to radically rethink their business model and project this decisiveness into the future. In its recent annual report[8] on the state of the legal sector, Altman Weil asked a future-defining question.

> *"Amid a global pandemic and a stalled economy, firm leaders are presented with an opportunity for another reset – an opportunity to truly rethink what a law firm ought to be doing to meet the needs of a marketplace that has already changed... Will law firms respond by rethinking their methods and structures to align with clients'? History says that most will not. Will this time be different?*

But remember, this is the time law firms took unprecedented decisions at lightning speed to fundamentally rethink how they should operate, resulting in 15-year highs when it comes to key measures of profitability and success. To lose the opportunity to harness this experience would be tragic. So ultimately, the question law firms leaders should be asking themselves, if not now, when?

2. Focus on strategic planning, not just financial planning

For most law firms, planning continues to be a financial exercise first and a strategic exercise second. Therefore, it's not hard to imagine that, under the current circumstances, law firm leaders wish to first focus on their financials instead of thinking more strategically.

However, when we once again look at the recent significant economic success of law firms over the past 16 months, there is a strong argument to put strategic planning first. Doing so unearths a number of once unthinkable opportunities to substantively drive firm profitability.

Take, for example, the dramatic shift to working from home. While this shift in the approach to the workplace for most law firms did reflect the underlying trend of most of their clients, the need for partners to radically rethink traditional models of how lawyers and staff operated should not be underestimated. Moreover, despite the fact that many partners may wish to get back to the office and return to the old office model, this is one area where a different strategic mindset may be extremely helpful.

A recent survey by Cushman and Wakefield[9] looked at the impact of the pandemic upon commercial real estate and projected that there would be a 20 percent reduction in office space in the next two years, a doubling in the amount of remote workers, and an increase in the number of agile workers by close to 50 percent. Add to this the fact that 98 percent of workers want a more agile approach to working and without question the future of work has changed.

The question for law firms of course is can they strategically adjust to a change like this? Can they plan for a future where offices in major urban/commercial centers become less important, where employees occasionally attend smaller remote or suburban offices, where financial discipline needs to be managed remotely, and where firm culture is built through online tools rather than staff meetings?

This is only one example of the bigger strategic shifts that are occurring as a result of the pandemic. But what is important to recognize, is that while these shifts can deliver significant financial benefits, they are a result of open-minded strategic planning, not financial planning.

3. Harness new-found partner cohesion to drive further change and deliver better results

In my ten plus years as chief marketing officer for a Big Four firm, and the world's largest law firm, driving partner collaboration to make tough decisions was always the most significant challenge. Will the COVID-19 pandemic change the way law firm partners operate, and will they take their new-found cohesion to push for the strategic shifts needed to excel in the post-COVID-19 future?

As we can see from some of the dramatic changes adopted by law firms, there is no doubt that the COVID-19 crisis has created a new partnership dynamic leading to stronger cohesion around tough decisions. Ultimately, partnerships have come closer together and worked harder at delivering success during the pandemic than at any time in the past 15 years.

The question now is can this continue, or will a stronger than expected financial performance over the past 18 months mask the need for continued change? Will partners instead heave a collective sigh of relief and grasp at the desire to go back to the old ways of inertia?

If law firm leaders revert to traditional financial models, then it is highly likely that this new visionary partner cohesion will be lost. If instead these leaders embrace the opportunity to first plan strategically, then the possibilities to drive further change and deliver better long-term results are potentially endless.

4. Double down on technology solutions to deliver efficiency and growth

Arguably, no single sector has benefited more from the COVID-19 pandemic than the technology sector. For lawyers who are known for their resistance to technology, COVID-19 has forced a reconciliation with technology as a must for productivity as well as client engagement.

According to a recent survey,[10] 84 percent of partners expected their firms to increase investments in technology. This is not to say that resistance to future change will disappear, but the experience of adapting to the radically changed market conditions in 2020 may well create more openness to experimentation in other forms of service delivery.

Moreover, there are further positive signs that lawyers expect the adoption of many of the pandemic-related technologies to continue, with 94 percent expecting to continue to use video meetings, 87 percent embracing remote desktop software, 41 percent using team chat software, and 28 percent benefiting from other collaboration tools.[11]

While this positive adoption of new technologies is a great step forward for partners, the challenge is how to convert this into adoption of firm-wide systems like fully integrated CRM systems, integrated marketing automation, client-friendly financial tools and so on. For example, if partners can successfully make that leap to new CRM systems and processes, which are historically difficult to implement with widespread adoption, then this action alone will have made all the COVID-19 pain worthwhile.

Once again, the ability to think strategically, harness partner cohesion and take the decisive action will be essential when it comes to doubling down on technology solutions.

5. Capture savings and invest in areas that made sense to cut, but now make sense to grow

There's a famous phrase in marketing circles: "I know that 50 cents of my marketing dollar is working, just not which 50 cents". Arguably this axiom could equally be applied to all other core business operations, whether they are IT, operations, finance, or HR.

As a result of COVID-19, many law firms took dramatic action and made significant cuts to their operating budgets. According to a recent survey,[12] law firm budgets were cut across the board, but the most dramatic cuts came in office expenses (-22.5 percent), recruiting (-40 percent), professional development (-42.1 percent) and marketing (-44 percent). As we have noted, the impact of these cuts, along with a number of other contributing factors, have driven PPP to the highest levels seen in 15 years.

One of the ancillary benefits of these cuts is that law firm leaders can, potentially for the first time, get a real sense of which 50 cents are working for them and which 50 cents, when cut, have no discernable negative impact on the firm's clients, business, revenue, or profitability.

For example, did the budget savings due to the limitation of business travel, attendance at international conferences, or hosting in-person marketing events have any discernable impact on revenue generation? Did hesitancy in hiring new senior practice leaders mean clients were lost, or new clients not won? Did investment in desktop video technology result in weaker or deeper client relationships?

Undertaking a strategic review of these budget cuts as well as investments is vital when preparing for the post-COVID-19 future – not only to understand where money can continue to be saved, but also where more money should be spent in the future.

For example, if remote working was successful, then it makes sense to plan strategically to move out of large urban offices into suburban structures and invest more in remote technology. If virtual video technology resulted in more frequent face-to-face client meetings, then reallocate monies from client travel to better desktop connectivity. If cutting cocktail events had no discernable negative impact, reallocate funds to thought leadership and content marketing programs.

6. Identify and invest in areas of business growth

Synonymous with reallocating savings towards new smart areas for investment is the need to identify the sectors that will create future business growth.

For many firms, this reallocation of resources away from traditional areas of revenue success towards new ones can be amongst the most challenging. For example, law firm leaders often find it very challenging to tell practice leaders or a group of lawyers operating in a specific specialty that this year they're reallocating marketing and practice budgets to other areas with higher growth prospects.

To embrace this opportunity, leaders need to not only harness their ability to once again make decisive decisions, they should spend the time to strategically plan for the areas of post-COVID-19 growth.

One way to do this is to take cost savings from other areas and invest in stronger market and business intelligence capabilities, as well as practice management. These groups can bring the insights that are most able to support managing partners in their arguments of why the firm needs to redirect existing budgets.

In addition to internal resources, a number of external consultancies are already looking at the practices and sectors most likely to grow in the post-COVID-19 world. For example, a few of those growth areas that have been identified include:

- Bankruptcy and restructuring;
- Cyber risk;
- COVID-19 litigation;
- Corporate Governance;
- Corporate social responsibility, including diversity;
- Employment law; and
- Vaccines and privacy.

7. Harness new ways of working to build teams, motivate staff, and build a stronger firm for the future

By now you may have heard of the term "The Great Resignation" – an idea first articulated by Texas A&M University professor Anthony Klotz.[13] This concept identifies a potential risk for employers as they seek to reopen post-pandemic and employees either resign rather than physically go back to work, or as the economy improves act upon their pent-up desire for a new opportunity.

While there are questions about whether resignations will materialize as envisioned, a number of statistics suggest that law firms should be wary. For example, 40 percent of people sampled as part of a recent Microsoft survey[14] said they wanted to change their jobs in 2021. In April, the share of US workers leaving jobs was 2.7 percent, according to the US Labor Department – the highest level since at least 2000.

Add to this general market trend the fact that the legal profession does not score well in terms of looking after employee wellbeing. A recent study by Bloomberg Law[15] found that 69 percent of respondents felt that the legal profession was not prepared to address employee wellbeing. Even when asked about their own firm experience, 40 percent felt that their own firms weren't prepared to address their wellbeing.

These trends are sobering for law firm leaders. However, rather than being afraid of what the post-pandemic workforce will look like, law firm leaders should embrace the changes that seemed to have worked so well for them over the past 18 months, rather than push for the old ways of working.

Law firm partners, lawyers, and staff have illustrated that they can handle remote working and, in response, firms have invested in enabling technologies and still increased profitability. Firms have found numerous ways to improve firm culture without resorting to staff meetings or annual partner retreats. Budget cuts have created pools of monies to be invested in new ways to support staff in a virtual world.

Embracing remote working, law firms don't have to lose their culture; there are many ways to continue to build it. These can be as simple as hosting a virtual lunch and buying staff food to be delivered, improved online coaching, support in mindfulness, or even giving people more flexibility in their work environments.

Ultimately, taking the time to understand what partners and staff want is important. The resulting thoughtful post-COVID-19 people strategy can not only save the firm money, but also help develop a more stable, happier team while enhancing profitability.

Conclusion

The restrictions and lockdowns that have characterized the COVID-19 pandemic have been a time of great stress and dislocation, and for far too many a period of huge loss. Consequently, there is a deep desire to go back to "normal", or to "the way it was before". For those law firm leaders and lawyers that realize a return to normal is exactly the wrong approach, there is an opportunity to create a brighter future where work–life balance, market innovation, and smart use of technology will define the law firm of the future. There is an opportunity to not let a good crisis go to waste.

References

1. *2020 Law Firm Benchmarks*, Bloomberg Law, July 2020.
2. *Ibid.*
3. *Ibid.*
4. *2021 Report on the State of the Legal market*, Thomson Reuters Institute, 2021.
5. *Reimagining the post-COVID-19 return*, Kevin Sneader, Bob Sternfels, McKinsey & co, 1 May 2020.
6. "40 times Trump said Coronavirus would go away", *Washington Post*, 2 November 2020.
7. *2021 Report on the State of the Legal market*, Thomson Reuters Institute, 2021.
8. "Law firms in transition 2020", Altman Weil, June 2020.
9. *Global Office Impact Study and Recovery Timing Report*, Kevin Thorpe, Cushman and Wakefield, 2020.
10. *2021 Report on the State of the Legal market*, Thomson Reuters Institute, 2021.
11. *2020 Law Firm Benchmarks*, Bloomberg Law, July 2020.
12. *2021 Report on the State of the Legal market*, Thomson Reuters Institute, 2021.
13. Bloomberg BusinessWeek, May 2021: www.bloomberg.com/news/articles/2021-05-10/quit-your-job-how-to-resign-after-covid-pandemic.
14. *Why the great resignation is greatly exaggerated*, Jack Kelly, Forbes, 8 June 2021.
15. *2020 Law Firm Benchmarks*, Bloomberg Law, July 2020.

Chapter 4:
The pandemic – a Trojan Horse for advancing diversity and inclusion?

By Patricia K. Gillette, author and inspirational speaker

The pandemic has wreaked havoc on so many aspects of our lives. The way we work; the way we play; the way we interact with each other; the way we think about friends and family. For over a year, we have been reinventing life, as we respond to this virus that seems like something from a science fiction (or horror) movie. Professionally and personally, our sense of time has blurred, with little demarcation between work hours and personal time, weekday and weekend as this virus shows its power to disrupt and destroy our definition of "normal". At the same time, we have had what some would call an "awakening" – driven in large part by the Black Lives Matter movement – to the longstanding and unaddressed disparities that adversely impact racial and ethnic groups. This has thrust diversity into the limelight, resulting in a renewed focus on the inequities that continue to plague our society.

The legal industry is not immune from the impact of these events. Indeed, there is no denying that this virus has had an immediate and radical affect on how lawyers in law firms do their work. Concepts that were previously considered "women's" issues – such as remote work, part-time work, and flexible work – have been catapulted into the mainstream of law firm life. Diversity and inclusion commitments that were often window dressing on firm websites or retreat agendas have become topics of everyday conversation. For the first time in decades, we see firms actually considering drastic changes in the way they think about the future composition of their workforce and the construction of their business models.

Can firms use this momentum to move diversity initiatives forward? Does it make business sense? Will it work? The answer? If not now, when? We have a moment in time to push for and possibly achieve change in an industry that has been tethered to traditional norms of what allegedly makes firms and lawyers successful. Women and diversity thought leaders have advocated for decades that the outdated law firm model and culture has to have change and this pandemic, coupled with the social movements that have accompanied it, may finally push these efforts over the top.

Using remote work models to advance diversity goals

We know that, despite the many efforts to level the playing field of responsibilities for childcare, women continue, as they have for decades, to bear more of these responsibilities than their male spouses or partners. Before the pandemic, this was one of the main challenges in advancing and retaining women in the workforce. But since the pandemic, this burden on women has become monumental. A study conducted by Roberta Liebenberg and Stephanie Scharf for the American Bar Association[1] drives home this point:

> *"The pandemic has exacerbated the already-disproportionate childcare burden on women lawyers. We asked those lawyers with dependent children at home about their childcare responsibilities before the pandemic and at the time of the Survey. We found a significant gender effect in both time frames: women were significantly more likely than men to have personal responsibility for childcare both before and during the pandemic. In addition, women were significantly more likely to have taken on more childcare responsibility during the pandemic. That increased responsibility for childcare is especially pronounced for women with pre-school children or children aged six through 13."*

This is the harsh result of the havoc the pandemic has wreaked on women lawyers in particular.

However, there is a valuable lesson that has come out of this pandemic and that may inure to the benefit of women and diverse lawyers – we now know that law firms can turn on a dime when necessary. Think about it. In a matter of weeks, firms responded to the pandemic by forcing law firms to do something they had resisted for years – allowing attorneys to work from home full-time; to perform work when it fit within their schedules (e.g. flexible work hours); to switch to part-time schedules to accommodate temporary personal needs. Granted, there wasn't really an alternative to these changes in the way work could be done because of the health risks associated with the pandemic. But the fact remains that firms adapted and changed course and by doing so – perhaps unintentionally – embraced the mantra that women's initiatives have been repeating for decades – that an attorney doesn't have to be in the office to be personally productive and for the firm to be profitable. And now we have statistics from 2020 that bear this out:

> *"Law firms are coming off of an especially profitable 2020. Across more than 130 surveyed firms, net income growth was up an average 9.9% in*

> *2020, as firms cut discretionary expenses for things like travel and events. That compares with 2019, when it rose by just 3.9%. Net income rose even higher for Am Law 50 firms in 2020: a 12.7% increase, resulting in an average 11.2% increase in profits per partner, according to the Wells Fargo survey."*[2]

Thus, the excuse often used by law firm leaders to reject changes in the way work gets done has been proven false – at least for now – and that has led several firms to finally formalize and institutionalize remote working arrangements. An August 2021 article published in the *Wall Street Journal*[3] highlighted some of the firms that are implementing various kinds of arrangements where lawyers can work remotely after the pandemic and into the future:

- Greenberg Traurig will allow lawyers to choose among its 30 office locations in the US to perform their work, regardless of where they are living;
- Akin Gump doesn't expect lawyers to work a five-day office workweek and is offering flexibility on work locations; and
- Nixon Peabody is allowing its lawyers to work on a fully remote basis.

Now, however, we must address the elephant in the room. Will these kinds of new working arrangements help advance diversity in law firms? That is a bit of an unknown. Left unmonitored, remote work can have a detrimental effect on diversity as it limits visibility for attorneys who take advantage of such programs and the data suggests that this may be primarily women. The reality is that absence does not make the heart grow fonder, and without formal systems and monitoring programs in place, remote workers can be easily ignored and forgotten, thus allowing implicit biases to kick in when decisions are being made for growth and advancement opportunities.

If remote work arrangements are going to become more widely accepted, firms should put in place formal systems to ensure that all their lawyers are getting the opportunities they need to advance within the firm.

The kinds of proactive steps a firm should consider include the following:

- **Assignment monitoring.** Firms should establish a checklist of the types of skills attorneys must have to advance within the firm. For litigators, that might be taking and defending depositions, arguing motions at the trial court level, participating in a trial, etc. Once that checklist is established, firms can monitor the skill sets that an attorney is developing and those for which he/she/they needs exposure to or further development. The firm would then have a system in place to make sure the attorney is put into the pipeline to receive those kinds of assignments. While this seems like a simple task, firms have resisted this type of solution and, as a result, assignments for growth opportunities are often given to white males over women and diverse attorneys due to many factors, including implicit bias. Monitoring assignments with an eye toward ensuring all attorneys have the same opportunities begins to address this inequity and is necessary for attorneys working remotely.

- **Pitch monitoring.** Client demand for diversity has increased the sensitivity of many firms to the need to present diverse teams for new client opportunities. Some firms simply ignore this, whilst others respond by sending the same women or diverse attorneys over and over again for these opportunities, as if there is only one woman or one diverse lawyer who is suitable for these pitches. Firms can break that cycle by keeping track of attorneys who are chosen to work on pitches and attend them. Clearly, not every attorney is suited for these types of opportunities. But, most attorneys, with some training and encouragement, can rise to the occasion if given the chance. Monitoring these pitch opportunities to ensure that women and diverse attorneys are represented and included is critical to their development. Again, remote working demands this type of systemic approach to cure the "out of sight, out of mind" issue that adversely affects such workers.
- **Succession planning.** With firms that have large institutional clients, succession planning is critical – not only to ensure the continuation of the relationship into the future, but also to ensure that those chosen as "successors" to the relationship include women and diverse attorneys. Bringing those attorneys into an institutional relationship early on in their careers can establish credibility and begin to build the trust necessary to position these attorneys to continue the relationship into the future. It is just good business to put in place systems to provide for the transition of institutional clients, but these systems should be monitored to ensure that women and diverse attorneys are represented and integrated into these institutional relationships. In a remote working environment, this becomes even

more important, as partners must create opportunities that raise the visibility of potential successors.

- **Leadership grooming.** There are many ways that attorneys are groomed for leadership positions in firms. Mentors and sponsors play important roles in developing leaders and those kinds of interactions become even more important in a remote work setting. Additionally, in remote work environments, the lack of day-to-day interactions can keep remote working attorneys off the radar as potential leaders. That is why institutionalizing leadership grooming is necessary. One way to do this is to put a system in place whereby the firm formally identifies attorneys, early on, who have leadership or business development skills and provides them with opportunities to practice those skills within the firm and with the work they do for clients. The *Mansfield Rule*,[4] which requires that one third of those being considered for leadership positions be women and diverse lawyers, provides a framework to not only ensure diversity in the choices of these future leaders, but also expands the pipeline by giving women and diverse attorneys visibility that they may not otherwise have.

None of these ideas is new. In fact, these are the kinds of systemic changes that thought leaders have been advocating for years because they address some of the root causes of the inequities that have historically existed in our firms. The formalization of remote work environments provide the impetus for institutionalizing these kinds of monitoring processes. And the adoption of these types of formal systems will inure to the benefit of women and diverse attorneys, whether they work remotely or not.

Remote working arrangements and flexible work hours appear to be here to stay. Firms that embrace these new concepts with the appropriate proactive measures in place will increase their chances of making our profession more attractive and conducive to the lifestyles of the men and women in our firms. But these work–life changes also provide a vehicle for implementing new systems that will help ensure that opportunities are evenly distributed to all lawyers regardless of gender, race, age, sexual orientation or any other factors, thereby addressing some of the barriers that have blocked opportunities for women and diverse attorneys in the past.

Using the momentum of social movements to advance diversity

In addition to the potential systemic changes that may come about in the name of adopting remote work as an alternative to the current law firm model, the social climate also provides an opportunity – and, actually, a necessity – for firms to re-up their commitment to increasing diversity in our firms. Will firms rise to occasion? That remains to be seen, notes Stephanie Scharf, name partner at Scharf Banks Marmor LLC and principal at law firm consultancy The Red Bee Group:

> *"We are going to see whether diversity and inclusion initiatives are in the DNA of law firms or whether those firms view them as just discretionary."*[5]

For too many years, firms have given lip service to diversity initiatives. Making the list, getting the seal of approval, and having the right words and pictures on a firm website have often taken the place of meaningful progress for diverse attorneys in our profession.

> *"Even after George Floyd's murder last year sparked a wave of activism and soul-searching throughout the United States, 16 of the nation's largest law firms, nine of which are in the Am Law 200, do not have even one Black partner in their partnerships. Despite having zero Black partners, many of these firms rank relatively high on The American Lawyer's 2021 Diversity Scorecard,*[6] *underscoring the uneven effect of efforts across the industry to bring in more attorneys of color."*[7]

That is not how it has to be. Noting what happened with the overnight adoption of remote working, Michelle Silverthorn, founder and CEO of Inclusion Nation said: "*…we were able to transform the workplace overnight when it came to Coronavirus. We can do the same when it comes to racism.*"[8]

Can we do as Ms Silverthorn suggests? That is, capitalize on this moment of change in the legal industry to correct the racial inequities that have existed in our firms for years? Can we use this apparent appetite for change to advance meaningful diversity initiatives in law firms? Hopefully yes, we can and, in fact, we are seeing some progress there:

> *"Studies have shown that because of the pandemic, many firms used the money saved on in person training events to hold virtual events on diversity and inclusion. And these events were better attended than in previous years because of the ability of lawyers to sign on at a convenient time."*[9]

Furthermore, while many feared that DEI budgets would be cut in response to the pandemic, that did not happen.

> *"...a recent survey conducted by Legal Talent Advisors[10] showed that nearly 50% of respondents stated their firms' commitment to DEI efforts stayed the same while 42.5% reported their firms expanded their efforts in 2020. The survey also found that 55% of respondents reported their firm's DEI budgets remained the same while 30% saying it increased. Less than 3% had their budgets frozen. and 2.5% saw a reduction in their DEI budgets."[11]*

This bodes well for DEI initiatives going forward, providing the pressure to recognize and correct the racial and ethnic inequalities that have plagued the legal industry continues. Remote work facilitates partners working with associates in different offices. That gives attorneys in "satellite" offices or in offices with larger diversity opportunity to work with partners on matters they would never have been considered for before due to their location. Other firms have encouraged partners to take a certain number of hours each month to reach out to diverse attorneys on a regular basis – thus increasing the visibility and familiarity of these attorneys. That has been tried before, but without success. However, with the ease of virtual settings, there has been increased participation by partners in these efforts. While interactions like these may seem small, they help to break down biases, presumptions, and other barriers to diversifying work teams.

System-wide changes are also on the rise as firms are beginning to recognize and appreciate the value of approaching diversity challenges as a business necessity, not simply a feel-good exercise. In this regard, there are several things that firms can do at this time to capture the spirit of change and use it to advance real movement on diversity. For example, firms should hire a chief diversity officer (CDO) who is a professional in this area and knows not only how to identify systemic barriers to the retention and advancement of diverse attorneys in law firms, but also how to develop impactful solutions to these barriers. This CDO should be on the executive committee and should report to the chair of the firm. The CDO must also have staff and monetary resources as well as the clearly articulated support of senior firm management.

Firms should also be initiating programs to identify pockets of inequality within their ranks. This is done by conducting a full-scale analysis of everything from recruiting efforts to work assignments, to advancement within the associate ranks, to promotion to partner and everything that comes with those milestones in an attorney's career. If inequities are discovered, then the root cause should be identified. Is it the lack of formal assignment systems? The absence of meaningful performance reviews?

The ineffectiveness of mentoring or sponsorship programs? Outright discrimination? Once those root causes are identified, then solutions can be implemented.

The power of role models in significant positions within the firm also cannot be overstated. It is critical for firms to realize that diversity initiatives alone cannot move the dial. There must be leadership from the top in terms of messaging around an inclusive culture that reflects a more diverse community within the firm. There must also be an increase in diversity in the leadership ranks so that women and diverse attorneys considering applying to the firm and those in the firm can see leaders who look like them in positions of power. This should not be a hard sell, as studies show that diversity in the rooms where power is wielded makes for better decision-making and better outcomes for the firm. Using the momentum of this time to seriously commit to the aforementioned Mansfield Rule and/or other ways of immediately impacting the composition of the leadership of the firm is a must.

Overall, the pandemic has provided opportunities for law firms to think anew about how work gets done, who does it, and when it gets done. It has spurred firms to make changes that before now seemed impossible and yet, have proved not only to be doable but be advantageous. The social movements that have presented the naked truth about the inequities of our society have not gone unnoticed by firms. Lawyers should use this moment of awakening to make change. Because, to quote Martin Luther King, "there is a fierce urgency of now". Let's not waste it.

References

1. Roberta Liebenberg and Stephanie Scharf: *Practicing Law in the Pandemic and Moving Forward*, American Bar Association, July 2021: www.americanbar.org/content/dam/aba/administrative/digital-engagement/practice-forward/practice-forward-survey.pdf
2. Andrew Maloney: "After Profits Soared in 2020," *The American Lawyer*, February 2021: www.law.com/americanlawyer/2021/02/01/after-profits-soared-in-2020-firms-optimistic-about-revenue-uptick-this-year/
3. Te-Ping Chen: "Lawyers Want to Bill More of Their Hours From the Sofa," *Wall Street Journal*, 7 August 2021: www.wsj.com/articles/covid-19-law-firm-work-from-home-11628254526?mod=searchresults_pos1&page=1
4. https://wikitia.com/wiki/Mansfield_Rule
5. www.law360.com/articles/1403826/hybrid-work-models-are-key-to-gender-parity-in-law-firms
6. www.law.com/americanlawyer/2021/05/24/the-2021-diversity-scorecard-ranking-the-legal-industry/

7. Dylan Jackson and Justin Henry: "Despite all that happened Last Year, Many Law Firms Still Have No Black Partners," *The American Lawyer*, 25 May 2021: www.law.com/americanlawyer/2021/05/25/despite-all-that-happened-last-year-many -law-firms-still-have-no-black-partners
8. *Ibid.*
9. Sharon Meit Abrahams: "Did the Pandemic Set Back the DEI Clock", Thompson Reuters, 25 March 2021: www.thomsonreuters.com/en-us/posts/legal/practice-innovations-april-2021-dei-pandemic/
10. www.legaltalentadvisors.com
11. Sharon Meit Abrahams: "Did the Pandemic Set Back the DEI Clock", Thompson Reuters, 25 March 2021: www.thomsonreuters.com/en-us/posts/legal/practice-innovations-april-2021-dei-pandemic/

Chapter 5: Law firms of the future (and other legal business models)

By Yvonne Nath, consultant, LawVision and CEO, ALSP Advisor

"A business model describes the rationale of how an organization creates, delivers, and captures value."[1]

Reduced to the most elementary definition, law firms are business entities formed by one or more lawyers to engage in the practice of law. While the basics of practicing law have remained largely static over time, the business of law has evolved steadily and – more recently – rapidly based on the demands of key stakeholders, which include clients, talent, lawmakers, and suppliers to the legal market and supported by technological advancements that allow us to work smarter and expand our global reach. For these reasons, we are at a juncture where the pressures on the traditional law firm business model are increasing from all sides, squeezing and shaping traditional law firms to evolve as well as making space in the market for new and different entrants to compete. Viable business models of legal service providers that go beyond the traditional law firm model can and do exist. In this chapter, I discuss some of the established and emerging business models for law firms and other companies providing legal services.

A brief overview of the evolving law firm model in the United States

What is a traditional law firm, anyhow? Today, there are over 150,000 law firms in the United States[2] if we define a law firm as a business entity formed by one or more lawyers to engage in the practice of law. The vast majority of these law firms today are sole practitioners and small firms not unlike the law firms that existed in the late 19th century when the largest law firms had only a handful of attorneys. Over the course of the 20th century, as US corporations grew in size and their legal matters grew in complexity, they began to outsource more of the legal work to law firms, many of which, in turn, grew in size to support their clients' increasing legal needs. These law firms often modelled their growth after the Cravath

System,[3] with a pyramidal talent structure that has a few partners at the top supported by many partner-track associates. This model succeeded for much of the 20th century. By the late 1980s, however, corporate leaders began to scrutinize their growing legal costs and sought to reduce legal spend by taking back some of this work to be performed internally. To do this, they grew their in-house law departments and pushed for improvements in internal law department operations (aka "legal operations"). GE's then-general counsel Ben Heineman[4] is considered to be the pioneer for legal operations in the industry. During his tenure, he eventually grew GE's law department to about 1,000 attorneys, which rivals some of the largest law firms in existence. Now we have organizations such as the Corporate Legal Operations Consortium (CLOC) that have since carried the torch to bring legal operations mainstream. In addition, legal procurement – a function dedicated to the selection of outside legal services – is rapidly growing within the industry.

With the growth of in-house law departments, legal operations, and legal procurement, clients are applying more pressure to outside counsel to extract more value from them. This and other pressures are causing law firms that operate under traditional models to evolve.

Before we move forward to review some of the other pressures influencing the evolution of law firms and other service providers in the space, let's look at some of the law firm business models that have thrived in the last several decades. I like how Bruce MacEwan has categorized law firms and generally agree with the advantages and challenges he's identified for each. In the table overleaf, I provide a high-level overview of this information with some modifications.[5]

In addition to clients' growing law department size and purchasing power, other pressures are causing law firms and emerging competitors to innovate their business models – often because the old model simply cannot handle modern demands.

Pressures shaping legal service providers

Here are some of the other pressures that are shaping law firms and other NewLaw business models.

Clients demand more for less

As mentioned earlier, clients want more value, but value does not mean the same thing for every client. The value of a service is determined by the client. More value may mean the service is faster, less expensive, simpler, yielding better results as measured by their particular KPIs, new

Table 1: Law firm business models. Based on MacEwan, Bruce: *Tomorrowland: Scenarios for Law Firms beyond the Horizon.*

Law firm model	Traits	Advantages/ opportunities	Challenges
Global players	On three or more continents	Heft and depth of capabilities; brand recognition	Managerial complexity How many can the world use?
Capital markets firms	Headquarters in global financial centers; strong banking, finance, and securities practices	Relational and reputational barriers to entry permit incumbents to dominate	Heavy reliance upon investment bank clients Barriers to entry for firms not already in this space
Kings of their hill	Headquarters in national but not global destinations Clients are mid and upper market corporations, high net worth people	Embedded in local market	When clients grow outside the territory these firms dominate, these firms must grow or loosen their grip on these clients Maintaining position as larger firms open offices in their territory
Boutiques	Come in all sizes One exceptional practice area	Clear focus; can be more efficient and profitable with fewer distractions	Reputation can hang on founders and fade over subsequent generations Must maintain that clear focus
Category killers	Target one broad practice Acquisitive of talent and other firms in this space	Can attract top talent with niche expertise Can benefit from serious investment in process optimization	Must maintain that clear focus
Hollow middle	"Full service" Not go-to firms for any particular strength They sit between the high quality, high price firms and those that offer good enough quality and high value	Can offer a little bit of everything to clients	Need stronger differentiating value propositions
Integrated focus	External orientation (e.g. industry) Only have practices that support that orientation	Clear brand, clear purpose	Must maintain that clear focus

or novel, customized, convenient, more accessible, or reduces risk or cost. Furthermore, clients and organizations are combining their knowledge and purchasing power to derive more value from outside counsel. Now, law firms tend to spread their support to a vast number of clients, rather than pin their survival to supporting an important few. Their clients, in turn, are applying convergence programs to consolidate the number of outside legal service providers they use so they can simplify their support network and demand more value (in the clients' eyes) from providers that want to win their high volume and high value (in the providers' eyes) work. And so goes this tug of war between clients and law firms, with each depending on the other's support while also trying to balance the tension between them. Generally speaking, the law firms that handle complex work for price-insensitive clients (an elite few) and the firms and other providers that can reduce their prices to increase their margins and the volume of work they handle, will be the firms that can endure this strange sport.

A maturing legal market and a trend toward standardization and commoditization

In 1994, the late Ward Bower, an early consultant to the legal industry, listed the following characteristics of our maturing legal industry:[6]

- Fierce competition based on price;
- Diminished importance of the quality of services;
- Marginalization of ethical and professional standards associated with those services and with the profession generally;
- Greatly enhanced level of consumer (client) sophistication in all aspects of practice;
- Large numbers of supplier (law firm) consolidations and contractions;
- Evolution of trade or "brand names";
- Increased market segmentation into distinct practice areas;
- Supplier (law firm) differentiation and specialization;
- Geographic expansion to find so-called "new" or underserved markets; and
- Decreased legal and financial barriers to entry into the profession.

The legal market is in its maturity. In a mature market, services evolve from being bespoke to standardized and, ultimately, commoditized.[7]

As data maturity within the legal industry continues, legal services will increasingly be procured and delivered according to more rigorous data-driven standards. Businesses will be able to standardize, unbundle, and source components of work from multiple providers. The SALI (Standards Advancement for the Legal Industry) Alliance is one organization that's influencing the acceleration of the trend towards standardization and the commoditization of legal services by establishing a system for coding legal work, much like how billing codes are used in the medical profession. Reconfiguring the legal supply chain through digital transformation, right-sourcing (outsourcing, multi-sourcing, and more), and productization will change how we perform work and package and sell knowledge. Attorneys who proactively embrace the inevitable in this ever-maturing market have a host of tools they can use to reduce the time they spend on low-level work, enjoy more meaningful work, improve the competitiveness and profitability of their work, and experience a higher quality work–life balance.

Explosion of legaltech and ALSPs

The legaltech space has exploded in recent years. In the first nine months of 2019, for example, over $1.2bn had been invested in legaltech.[8] (To view a variety of legaltech companies in the market today, check out the Legal Technology Hub[9] directory of legaltech.) Similarly, the market for alternative legal service providers (ALSPs) has been growing. The ALSP market is now valued at around $14bn and is expected to see continued growth as law departments and law firms realize the tangible benefits of working with them. Some 79 percent of law firms surveyed by Reuters are using ALSPs to some degree, along with 71 percent of corporate law departments.[10] ALSPs have the advantage of lower cost labor, access to and expertise in legaltech, the ability to work 24/7, and effective process and project management skills. Law firms can gain a competitive advantage by working with ALSPs and learning to work like them.

Workers want work–life balance

Technological advancements, generational mindset shifts, and the recent pandemic have changed how, when, and where we can work. No longer confined to working from an office space during business hours, many professionals can now work from their laptops just about anywhere. In addition to being able to perform traditional jobs in new ways, new types of flexible job opportunities abound in the flexible staffing arena, gig economy, and online marketplaces.[11]

Changing law firm ownership regulations

Says Dan Rodriguez in Legal Evolution:

> *"In the United States, we operate in a constitutional orbit of legal services regulation which is constituted by fifty different state regulatory structures and schemes… there are some common rules – think of the ABA's Model Rules of Professional Conduct, standards for law school accreditation, and the Uniform Bar Exam."*[12]

Over time, in the US, on a state-by-state basis, we are seeing the relaxing of regulations around who can own and manage law firms. Arizona, Utah, and Florida were the first movers. More will follow.

Globalization and consolidation

Digitization and globalization have created the Information Age. Information is readily available and exchangeable. Mergers and acquisitions of law firms and other businesses, as well as professional networks, allow businesses to exchange more information and opportunities and to expand their geographic reach. Moreover, in a competitive, mature market, mid-size law firms can suffer from having overhead structures similar to that of their larger counterparts yet mid-size firms have a smaller market reach. Consolidation allows firms to benefit from economies of scale, access to lower-cost labor markets, widespread brand recognition, and the ability to support high value, complex cross-border matters.

Economic factors

The Great Recession did not change the legal industry as profoundly as many expected. However, it did accelerate underlying industry trends. Likewise, while the pandemic stifled some economic activity, some law firms had their best years yet. In fact, in the aftermath of the pandemic, we have seen a spike in transactional work and transactional practices fiercely competing for talent.

For a deeper analysis of the immediate and longer-term implications of the pandemic for law firms, I recommend *Guidance for Law Firm Leaders: The Legal Profession in a COVID-19 World*, published by LawVision.[13]

Other viable legal business models

A plethora of legal business models have emerged in response to these pressures. One could try to create a taxonomy of models, though I am seeing a blurring of lines among them as they mix and match traits in search of competitive advantages. Some models have similar or overlapping traits while others are more unique. In this Cambrian explosion, there's no one winner – different models can succeed. Likewise, many businesses under any one model can achieve varying degrees of success and many will fail. There are some interesting models in existence today. For this chapter, I have lightly brushed the surface of some models and provided a few points about each. This is not, however, a comprehensive survey of the legal business landscape.

Table 2: Other viable legal business models.

Legal business model	Traits	Advantages/ opportunities	Challenges	Examples
Legal talent stores/ marketplaces	Online databases of attorneys and other talent; sometimes visible, sometimes requiring a consultant in the middle to match the talent to the client/project Priced by the time increment or project; prices are visible up-front or revealed upon inquiry	Give buyers more options and control over who they hire Allow under-utilised talent to have more outlets, try different types of work, control their schedule	Forming teams; having consistent availability Can be redundant as some talent registers on multiple market-places	Hire an Esquire for seasoned attorneys gigLAW for law interns
Legal service stores/ marketplaces	A specific service can be purchased, often at a fixed price that is visible up-front to the buyer	Allow sellers' services to be easily searched and found by buyers Easier for buyers to comparison shop	Many sellers are not ready to make their pricing transparent Challenging to offer high-value and complex services on marketplaces, better suited for routine services	Notarise PartnerVine

continued on next page

Legal business model	Traits	Advantages/ opportunities	Challenges	Examples
Legal product stores/ marketplaces	A specific product can be purchased, usually at a fixed price that is visible up-front to the buyer Can also be a consumer products business that offers legal resources, not just a legal business	Automated/ streamlined sales and delivery; improved buyer experience (when done well)	Easier to compare information across providers and determine how much their offerings really differ Transparency accelerates commoditisation	PartnerVine WHSmith's LawPack offerings[14]
Incubators and freemium offerings targeted at start-ups	Have a subsidiary, affiliate, or team dedicated to supporting entry-level clients using lower-cost resources, often supplying products and services for free or at very low cost	By offering a little low-value work to start-ups and small clients, businesses can establish a relationship with clients early on. This may lead to clients sending them higher-value and volume of work over time	Requires up-front investment in businesses that may not survive long	Mischon de Raya's MDR Lab CooleyGO
Alternative Business Structure (ABS)/ non-attorney ownership and direction15	Relaxed restrictions around the ownership, direction, and practice of law Varies by jurisdiction	Can incentivise non-attorneys through equity awards Can accept outside investment, even go public	Regardless of ownership and direction, these are still businesses that operate in a competitive market and must generate returns for their owners/ investors	Gateley Big Four Pearson Butler
Multi-discipli-nary professional services firms	Combined legal and other professional services capabilities	Can offer a suite of resources to solve clients' business prob-lems (client needs aren't 100 percent legal and wearing a lawyer hat is not necessary for performing all of this work)	Coordinating multiple providers	Big Four Law firms with consulting arms (e.g., legaltech, lobbying)

continued on next page

Legal business model	Traits	Advantages/ opportunities	Challenges	Examples
Captive ALSP	An ALSP owned by a law firm (some are partially-owned by firms to permit outside investment)	Signals to clients that firms are looking for ways to provide more value Partially-owned ALSPs can be a good model for law firm legaltech subsidiaries seeking outside investment to scale	Cultural barriers to change when an innovative business is owned and directed by a traditional business Capital structure and incentive differences between partner-ship of firm and corporate model of captive	Waller Lansden Dortch & Davis' Clear Diligence Keesal, Young & Logan's KP Labs
Independent ALSP	An ALSP not owned by a law firm	Have been around longer than captives, more experience, well-defined processes and established systems Can operate under their own culture, not confined by law firm culture	As more ALSPs broaden their service offerings, they are becoming more like law firms and will face many similar challenges. Still, many law firms view ALSPs as competitors and do not trust them enough to work with them	Kalexius Integreon
Big Four	Accounting firms with global reach and law firm affiliations	Interconnected, global reach Access to technology, multi-disciplinary talent, information, large clients	Regulations and conflicts prevent them from monopolising the market May be hindered by high overhead and hierarchy or other cultural aspects	EY, Deloitte, PwC, KPMG

continued on next page

Legal business model	Traits	Advantages/ opportunities	Challenges	Examples
Virtual firms	No office space	Lower overhead Can more quickly and less expensively enter or exit new geographic markets	Cultural stickiness and effectiveness	Fisher Broyles
Flat firms (partner-only)	Leverage ALSPs and other outside resources rather than internal associates	Agile, lower fixed expenses Good model for partners at the end of their careers who want to harvest what they can without worrying about succession	Partners may still be involved in running the business, for better and worse May not mentor the next generation of talent	Flatiron Law; Fisher Broyles
Bifurcated practice and business management and support	The law practice is its own firm while business support is provided by separate non-law firm entities Like the MSO/DSO model in the medical and dental professions Business support may be provided by several different entities	The business support entity can receive outside investment and be owned by non-attorneys and managed by business professionals Shared service centers can benefit from economies of scale and lower overhead costs	Increases the divide between lawyers and non-lawyers Important for them to maintain trust and speak each other's languages to have effective working relationships	The late Atrium Partial separation: Allen & Overy's Legal Services Center (some separation, but not a pure bifurcation) Another partial example: UnitedLex and Elevate Flex rebadging of staff under their companies and leasing them back to law firms
More non-attorneys being hired within law firms	More business professionals and technologists and other support staff	Law firms with more non-attorneys may be operated more like a corporation and less like a partnership	Non-attorneys, unless they are also revenue generators or cost reducers, will add to the overhead costs of a firm and will have to otherwise demonstrate how they are adding value	Chief innovation officers, strategic account managers, pricing analysts, legal project managers, technologists, etc.

Exploring other legal business models in more depth

Let's explore a couple of these models by looking at specific businesses that are trying them.

A flat firm: Flatiron Law Group LLP

Flatiron is an M&A boutique law firm for private middle-market deals. It was founded in 2017 by former BigLaw partners. Flatiron is what I call a "flat" firm – it avoids the traditional pyramidal leverage model that requires many associates to support one partner. Instead, at Flatiron, partners leverage technology and ALSPs for support. Per its website, "We are a technology-leveraged law firm that applies digital deal tools, advanced analytics and best practices to close deals faster, better, with less risk and better outcomes".

Flatiron operates on a cloud-based practice platform, with an outsourcing (gig) labor model, and it's developed proprietary deal tools and methodologies to offer premium deal work on a principally fixed-fee basis. In a separate commercial company, it developed a digital deal platform it calls Deal DriverSM for its own use and for use by other M&A shops who seek to improve the deal process. Deal DriverSM essentially chaperones a seller's data through each step of an M&A deal and associates it with the critical seller deliverables (i.e. due diligence production and disclosure schedules).

Flatiron also offers due diligence and transaction support through a service it calls Deal Vision. It can offer these diligence services coupled with or uncoupled from traditional legal advisory services. This way, clients can choose to retain their legacy counsel for the advisory work and Flatiron for diligence, if they prefer.

When Flatiron outsources to ALSPs and other service providers, it manages the quality for the client. This oversight provides value to the client and is one reason why clients can benefit from having their law firms manage ALSPs rather than bypass their firms to work with ALSPs directly.

From its website:

> *"Flatiron recognizes that for some types of work, added low cost labor is needed to perform routine or repetitive tasks, supported by our technology, where appropriate. In those instances when human resources are the most efficient method to produce the requisite quality product required we utilize Legal Services Outsourcing (LSO) companies. We establish strategic partnerships with third-party legal service providers to work either directly with the client or client general counsel or in a tripartite relationship with both the client and its outside counsel. In all cases, the outsourcing goal is to improve efficiency and delivery times while maintaining (and depending on the type of work, improving) the quality of the work."*[16]

To manage quality control in the use of LSOs, documentation entered into by Flatiron and the LSO ensures a shared understanding of respective roles. Quality control encompass both risk management and commercial elements. Flatiron maintains control and makes sure the firm always has the precise information needed to manage the legal matter overall, except as may otherwise be agreed by Flatiron and the client.

To give you a flavor of how transactions can be handled in collaboration with ALSPs, see this diagram of how Flatiron handles an M&A deal.

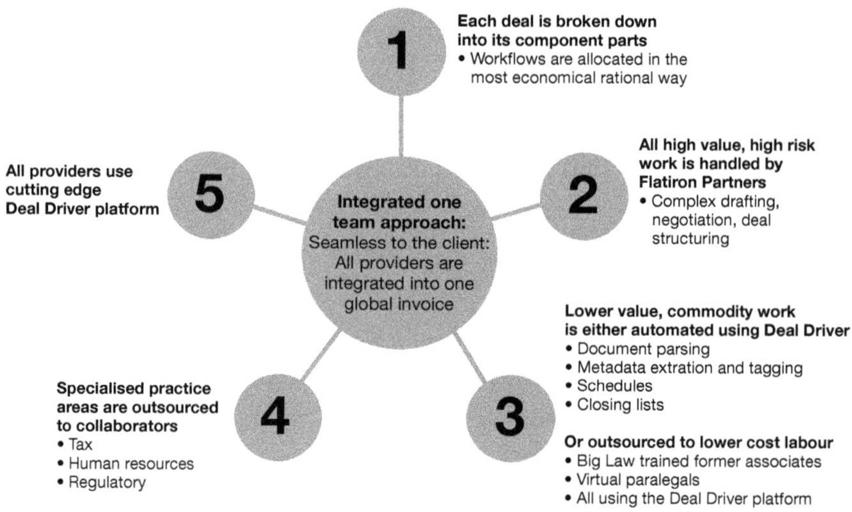

Figure 1: Flatiron Law Group LLP's deal model (reproduced with the permission of Flatiron).[17]

The partner-heavy flat firm can be a great model for partners who wish to harvest what they can from their practices at the tail end of their careers without worrying about supporting future generations of talent. However, Flatiron is not doing that. These partners are more interested in enjoying their practice today by focusing on the higher-value work and automating and outsourcing the lower-value work. It is building its legacy as an innovative law firm that attracts non-traditional talent and it is building technology for tomorrow so that, when it no longer practices, it can reap the dividends from the technology solutions it has built.

Non-attorney ownership: Pearson Butler

In 2007, the Legal Services Act of 2007 was passed in the UK, which opened the doors to non-attorneys for law firm ownership.[18] In the United

States, regulatory reform around law firm ownership if finally happening but on a state-by-state basis.

In August 2020, Arizona and Utah became the first US jurisdictions to relax restrictions around the practice of law. Specifically, Arizona approved outside ownership of law firms, while Utah launched a regulatory sandbox pilot program allowing nonlawyers to offer certain legal services.[19] In 2021, Florida followed. Other states like California, North Carolina, Illinois, and New York are considering ways to loosen restrictions around the provision of legal services.

Pearson Butler is a 30-attorney firm in Utah.[20] In March 2021, the firm received approval from the Utah Supreme Court to revise its ownership model. The information that follows was taken from its Amended Sandbox Authorization Packet from the Utah Office of Legal Services Innovation.[21]

Pearson Butler law firm is set up as one of three professional service entities, alongside a financial services firm and a registered investment adviser firm. The three are together owned by a holding company, itself owned by a combination of lawyers and non-lawyers. Here are some of the services their non-attorneys can provide:

- Preparing uncontested divorce paperwork;
- Assisting consumers with small claims paperwork;
- Filling out Chapter 7 bankruptcy forms;
- Wage claims;
- Disability;
- Immigration;
- Debt settlement;
- Collections;
- Form-based estate planning;
- Uncontested probate document preparation;
- The EEOC process, including appearing in administrative hearings;
- Unemployment hearings; and
- Family law document preparation, including uncontested custody and child support documents, uncontested divorce mediation documents, assisting with OCAP paperwork etc., preparing other documents for pro se litigants, including stipulations etc.

The firm's website has the following disclaimer:

> *"This law firm is owned by nonlawyers. Some of the people who own this law firm are not lawyers. This means that some rights and protections may be administered differently from attorney-owned law firms."*[22]

In conclusion

The explosion of legal business models that have evolved in response to myriad pressures both within and without the industry is exciting, but it can be tough to keep up with all this activity and know where to focus. In this chapter, I've chosen to highlight just a couple of the interesting legal business models that are in operation today and may emerge as winning models in the future. In my law firm strategy and legal operations consulting work, I help law firms and other legal service providers understand and navigate the changing landscape of the business of law. If you would like to learn more about any of these models or how your law firm can leverage alternative legal service providers and test new business models, I would be happy to tell you more.

References

1. Osterwalder, Alexander, and Pigneur, Yves. *Business Model Generation*. Hoboken, NJ, United States, Wiley, 2010.
2. Statista. "Legal Services Firms in US 2010-2018, by Size." *Statista*, 7 June 2021, www.statista.com/statistics/822038/us-legal-services-market-firms-size.
3. Wikipedia contributors. "Cravath System." *Wikipedia*, 10 May 2021, https://en.wikipedia.org/wiki/Cravath_System
4. Heineman, Jr. *The Inside Counsel Revolution: Resolving the Partner-Guardian Tension*. 2nd Printing, e-book, Ankerwycke, 2016.
5. MacEwan, Bruce. *Tomorrowland: Scenarios for Law Firms beyond the Horizon*. 1st ed., CreateSpace Independent Publishing Platform, 2017.
6. Berlin, Howard J., *et al*. "Facing the Inevitability, Rapidity, and Dynamics of Change." *Florida Bar Journal*, vol. 74, no. 3, 2000, p.12, www.floridabar.org/the-florida-bar-journal/facing-the-inevitability-rapidity-and-dynamics-of-change.
7. Nath, Yvonne. "The Gig Is up and Coming (223)." *Legal Evolution*, 14 February 2021, www.legalevolution.org/2021/02/the-gig-is-up-and-coming-223.
8. Ambrogi, Bob. "At $1.2 Billion, 2019 Is A Record Year for Legal Tech Investments – And It's Only September." *LawSites*, 16 September 2019, www.lawsitesblog.com/2019/09/at-1-1-billion-2019-is-a-record-year-for-legal-tech-investments-and-its-only-september.html.
9. "Legaltech Hub." *Legaltech*, 2021, www.legaltechnologyhub.com.

10. The Center on Ethics and the Legal Profession at Georgetown Law, *et al.* "Alternative Legal Service Providers 2021." *Thomson Reuters*, 2021, www.thomsonreuters.com/en-us/posts/legal/alsp-report-2021.
11. Nath, Yvonne. "The Gig Is up and Coming (223)." *Legal Evolution*, 14 February 2021, www.legalevolution.org/2021/02/the-gig-is-up-and-coming-223.
12. Rodriguez, Dan. "Our Bar Federalism, Part I (239)." *Legal Evolution*, 4 July 2021, www.legalevolution.org/2021/07/our-bar-federalism-part-i-239.
13. LawVision, *et al. Guidance for Law Firm Leaders: The Legal Profession in a COVID-19 World*. Independently published, 2020.
14. www.whsmith.co.uk/search?q=legal&cgid=ALL,10 July 2021.
15. "The Sandbox Grows, and So Do Outside Investors for Law Firms." *The American Lawyer*, 1 June 2021, www.law.com/americanlawyer/2021/05/28/the-sandbox-grows-and-so-do-outside-investors-for-law-firms.
16. https://flatiron.legal/engagement-model/#LegalProcessManagement
17. Flatiron Law. "Deal Model – Flatironlaw." *Flatironlaw – A Better Way to Do Deals*, 12 July 2021, flatiron1.moldave-cook.com/deal-model.
18. For a study on the impact of this regulatory reform, see Center for Strategy and Evaluation Services, "Impact Evaluation of SRA's Regulatory Reform Programme," April 2018. https://www.sra.org.uk/globalassets/documents/sra/research/abs-evaluation.pdf
19. "Restrictions on Legal Services Loosened This Year. What Does That Mean for 2021?" *Law.Com*, 30 December 2020, www.law.com/2020/12/28/restrictions-on-legal-services-loosened-this-year-what-does-that-mean-for-2021.
20. "Utah Attorneys." *Pearson Butler*, 2021, www.pearsonbutler.com.
21. https://utahinnovationoffice.org/wp-content/uploads/2021/04/Auth-Packet-Amended-Pearson-Butler.pdf
22. "Utah Attorneys." *Pearson Butler*, 2021, www.pearsonbutler.com.

Chapter 6: The fledgling post-pandemic law firm – status quo or brand new normal?

By Mary Juetten, Singular Law Group

Earlier this year, while in my home office/master bedroom chatting with a fellow legal technologist over Zoom, we lamented the ongoing challenges of client-centric legal service delivery. He raised the possibility of doing things differently under Arizona state's October 2020 legislation that allows for alternative business structures (ABS), including non-lawyer[1] ownership. However, we immediately concluded that our goals must be more than just a different ownership structure, because that would be more of the same, just with different players. Instead, a new post-pandemic law firm should be designed around the business and technology savvy brought by the non-lawyers, and those who have worked outside of the legal profession, to support an approach that puts clients' needs and wants first. This chapter uses a case study approach to explore how we can keep the best of the status quo while building a new firm – Singular Law Group (SLG)[2] – that will absolutely delight our clients in a measurable manner, to become the model for the new normal.

Start with the end in mind

This mantra is a slight tweak from Stephen Covey's second habit of the seven for highly effective people, "Begin with the end in mind" and requires a clear vision of where we are going, before we start. Regardless of whether you are starting a professional services firm or a technology company, planning is the key to success. However, much more can be borrowed from the business world or the non-legal company, starting with setting company values and mission from day one.

One of our very first tasks before applying to the Arizona Supreme Court for the ABS license was to brainstorm how we wanted to build and run SLG. We knew what we did not wish to do, which is to perpetuate the status quo, the quintessential ivory tower law firm. We believe that the firm needs to be reinvented, based on some of the horror stories that we have heard or experienced firsthand. To illustrate, recently I have seen a lot of social media posts about how legal consultations should never be free. The comments from lawyers, which itself is a bit of an echo chamber, seem to center around attorney needs and wants instead of putting the focus on the client's fears, hopes, and requirement for assistance.

Further, I read a popular post on LinkedIn that described how an attorney set his rates solely based on what he needed to be profitable and escalated those rates each year, regardless of his clients' financial situation. This lawyer turned away anyone who questioned his rate or his value, or simply could not afford his service. As a business person, I understand the need to make money; however, if you cannot articulate the value that you add, you're simply not client-centric. If I am purchasing any service, I instinctively will consider the cost versus the benefit and if someone tells me that I cannot ask about the value to me as the customer, I would move on to the next provider.

What is client-centric?

The mission of SLG is to provide unique legal solutions to the underserved and marginalized, with a focus on the significant Hispanic population within Arizona, including the small business owner. Our approach relies heavily on technology and automation. This can only be achieved by putting the customer at the center of everything, which includes using a client success manager for each matter.

One of the most common problems cited by clients is a lack of communication from their lawyer. As a busy legal professional, I understand that you do not want to spend time on updates, particularly if there is nothing new to report. However, as a customer, I want to be apprised of what is going on in my legal matter. Over the years, I have had issues with legal and financial professionals who do not communicate in a timely manner with me as the client. Return the call or email; it's simple. Assigning a non-lawyer to take on administrative tasks, including passing on updates from the lawyer, provides the information bridge between the busy lawyer and the curious client.

In addition to communication, clients need to understand their legal matter and the process to resolution or to the desired outcome, regardless of the type of law. There is often an expectation gap or misalignment between what the client believes the process may entail and what various outcomes are possible versus the reality as known by the lawyer. It's our job as the expert to close that gap and ensure that the clients are not surprised. I know many lawyers who are lazy about holding clients' hands as they view it and feel that it is beneath them to explain the legal process.

I am quite confident that those same lawyers would demand details when they pay hard-earned money for services.

However, being client-centric does not mean giving away free time and advice. This is the place for virtual experience, including using technology that both educates the client and provides valuable information for the lawyer. The technology tools listed below are a few examples of software that give the potential client some legal information (not advice) to educate and help them with their issues or at least create a roadmap for resolution. On the lawyer side, the technology both triages and gathers intake information to save time and therefore money.

- An online self-guided legal checkup provided for businesses and individuals (such as Traklight).
- A bot that gathers information to do the company's incorporation documents to then be reviewed by a lawyer (such as LawDroid).
- A workers' compensation potential settlement calculator (such as that developed by ONE400).

The notion of nurturing clients with information and education instead of trying to immediately sell a specific legal solution is a refreshing approach to legal marketing borrowed from other industries. The client gains confidence by using the calculator or the legal checkup and discovers the issues, risks, and potential rewards.

In addition, firms need to be flexible with fees and providing options within limited scope representations. A popular approach is a low-cost subscription service where an individual or business pays a flat monthly fee to access a menu of services. At SLG we will offer this type of plan to small and micro businesses.

Our plan includes technology to automate common business processes and documents to increase efficiency and decrease costs to our clients. Attorneys at SLG will not be burdened by administrative tasks, so they can focus on creative problem solving that benefits their clients and provides the best representation possible to their clients. Additionally, SLG will use technology, as listed above, to help individuals and businesses be more informed about legal issues that concern them, before they engage a lawyer.

What is ABS?

The idea of non-lawyer ownership has been debated and discussed in the US for decades. Last year, two states acted. First, the state of Utah created an ABS sandbox approach as an experimental approach in the summer of 2020. In October, Arizona came out with a permanent regulatory and licensing structure for a variety of ABS entities.[3]

The state of Arizona's Supreme Court website defines an ABS as follows:

> *An ABS is an entity that provides legal services and has nonlawyer ownership, managers, or decision makers in the business. Nonlawyers could have economic ownership (an equity stake) in the business, but only lawyers and other individuals licensed or certified by the Arizona Supreme Court are permitted to provide legal services.*[4]

The application process allows for companies to create a range of offerings, from traditional law firms to non-law firms both small and large. Applicants can come from within Arizona, the other US states, or from outside the US, plus non-profit organizations are permitted.

Several other states are examining this idea of having non-lawyer ownership either on a trial basis like Utah or as a permanent license, subject to oversight and annual renewal, as Arizona has implemented. As a business owner, I would not wish to invest the considerable time and money required to apply for only a trial or pilot program. At the time of writing, our Arizona ABS application for SLG is not yet approved but it has been reviewed and this has taken several months. To apply as a new firm, we were required to provide our firm operating agreement and information on policies, processes, and governance. The application fees range from $2,000 to $12,000 and the annual fees are set at 50 percent of the original fee.

Why ABS?

The idea that the speed of innovation within the law can be accelerated with outside investment and allowing non-lawyers to run law firms should not be revolutionary, but that is where the US is today. Personally, I have known my future SLG partner for over eight years and he is both a savvy business person and marketer within the legal industry. Equally important, he understands the need for enabling technology and how to automate processes; he himself has developed legal subscription plan software.

The Arizona Supreme Court laid out regulatory objectives for all ABS applicants as follows:

- Protecting and promoting the public interest;
- Promoting access to legal services;

- Encouraging an independent, strong, diverse and effective legal profession;
- Advancing the administration of justice and rule of law; and
- Promoting and maintaining adherence to professional principles.

As we build SLG, we will use the list above as a touchstone for our plans but, truly, the second objective is of paramount importance and in our opinion should lead the list, with the others being supportive or secondary.

Again, the question is why is ABS even needed? Not directly tied to the pandemic but over the years spent selling technology to lawyers and running the innovation company Evolve Law, I have observed that lawyers do not usually make good business people. This is a bit of a generalization, but US attorneys are basically risk adverse and tend to focus on the practice of law as a craft. As "legal artists", there is a black box mentality and a resistance to letting go of simple tasks. I have experienced lawyers who insist that asking a client some basic yes or no questions about their business is the practice of law and cannot be replaced with a non-lawyer or technology.

To expand this idea, if lawyers are the only ones who can do everything within a firm, the price for those services is going to be high, and likely not accessible by the average potential client. The idea of an ABS for a traditional law firm is that meaningful input into the decisions and running of the business can be done by non-lawyers, along with outside investment to provide technology and more.

What does ABS mean for virtual firms?

Outside funding is critical for the growth of the client side of the virtual firm. The use of cloud-based technology for calendaring, practice management, billing and more administrative or lawyers' tasks is now commonplace and reasonably priced. The potential to have non-lawyer ABS owners contribute technology and funds will be a game-changer for the client.

Taking the expansion of the talent pool for management and the dollars for the firm a step further, with an ABS, the idea of being virtual should be common. Those operating professional firms outside of the law will be familiar with the client-centric model and understand the idea of leveraging technology and non-lawyer assistance, including virtual or remote workforce.

In addition, I find that non-lawyers are more open to new ideas than attorneys and willing to experiment. In Arizona, there is a new category of legal service provider called a Licensed Paraprofessional (LP) that launched this year. It appears to be met with a similar suspicion by lawyers as was the now defunct Limited License Legal Technician program in Washington State. At SLG we plan to hire some of the first graduates from the new LP program because it will be more affordable for our family law clients who have simple legal needs.

Getting started

A new firm should consider what clients need; consider the demand, not the supply. Below is the SLG approach for our go-to market strategy for Arizona that I share as an example of the required analysis. We researched and determined that there are a number of Arizonans who cannot access legal services due to:

- Geographical access;
- Language barriers;
- Americans with Disabilities (ADA) issues; and
- Affordability.

From day one, SLG plans to use technology, including Traklight's business and personal legal checkups (also in Spanish) to identify legal issues and triage the need for legal services. The software includes free education for businesses and the client dashboard includes a roadmap for legal and other services. This tool will be deployed on a mobile-friendly platform that can be accessed by any smart device (e.g., phone, tablet, laptop, desktop). Deploying this tool on the SLG website means that any Arizonan in any part of the state will have easy access to information that helps inform them about their potential legal issues that need to be addressed.

Additionally, SLG will communicate with prospective clients as well as clients via streaming video applications, phone, and encrypted SMS messaging services. By deploying such methods for communicating with SLG, there is essentially no geographical access limitation, thus allowing us to serve rural communities as well as those in denser metropolitan areas.

Arizona's Latino population is approximately 32 percent.[5] While most Latino households in AZ are English speakers, there are a great number of households that are not. SLG will be deliberate in its desire to meet the needs of these households by hiring bilingual administrative staff as well as bilingual attorneys, paralegals, and LPs. Although there are other non-English speaking populations in AZ, we will focus on Latinos at launch since it is the highest single minority group in the state.

According to the CDC, there are over 12 million Americans with visual disabilities.[6] The SLG website meets the website content accessibility guidelines standard so that people with visual impairments who access the web with specialized browsers can consume our content and engage with us online. We strongly believe that if you can't read legal information, then you don't have access to justice; SLG will adopt best practices and exemplify the changes needed to promote accessibility in the legal industry.

Being a virtual law firm that also uses technology to automate routine work, SLG will keep overhead and expenses low, while complying with the state's rules of professional conduct, specifically around conflict checking and lawyer involvement. Additionally, SLG will provide limited scope flat fee, subscription based, and commoditized legal services online so that Arizonans have more affordable options for acquiring legal services.

None of the above is unique to any law firm and can be used regardless of ownership or management structure.

Create a solid foundation

The legal values of professional independence, confidentiality, and conflict-free representation are at the core of the SLG culture. However, we will go beyond requirements to create a culture code that is inclusive from day one.

By way of example, the SLG team will embrace the following firm values:

- Integrity and honesty;
- Client-centric delivery;
- Transparency;
- Diversity and inclusion; and
- Teamwork.

As the firm grows, we will create goals and use stretch targets. As we do not use the billable hour, we will track the effort in terms of time, but our key performance indicators will focus on whether we added value to our clients, customer satisfaction, and accountability for financial results.

Build it and they will come?

Many start-ups have failed because they did not achieve a fit between the market and their product. Although there is a need for legal services, the notion that if we hang our shingle for SLG, clients will come, is a complete fallacy. As much as some lawyers would like to believe that providing legal services is some type of magical experience that cannot be understood by clients, we will be breaking our services down to simplify and focus on results for clients.

Our plan is to not actually build a bricks and mortar firm and instead build around clients' needs. We will strive to meet the clients where they wish to be served.

Virtual versus technology

Many lawyers are afraid of technology and, in the US, many still claim that they will not use the cloud for their practice. Meanwhile, the same lawyers use Google's email services, online payments, or a multitude of other applications where all the data resides in the cloud.

A true virtual firm means that there is no office for clients to visit nor is there a space for all of the team to meet. We work remotely from our houses or wherever. Being a virtual firm requires technology but some lawyers who have offices will try to avoid using it. However, to be client-centric, all lawyers must embrace technology regardless of whether they have an office or not.

How much virtual is too much?

Personally, I would be happy to provide services, whether legal or mediation, from anywhere in the world and never go to the office again. In fact, I would rather not even have an office! However, to be client-centric, a variety of pathways to legal help is important, including in-person.

Earlier this spring, we received several family law leads and engaged an attorney to perform any legal work as I am not a family law practitioner. This was a bit of an experiment as far as working with a lawyer who was not an employee but had an Of Counsel relationship with SLG. One of the first leads did not wish to meet over Zoom. He was older and felt more comfortable meeting in person. As we planned SLG to be virtual-only with respect to both business and family law offerings, we had to adjust and found space that we could rent by the hour for these meetings.

We must also honor the cultural differences of our clients. Some people do not wish to pay with a credit card, either online or over the phone. For those clients, it's not about convenience, rather it's cultural to come into an office and pay in cash when meeting with the lawyer. Based on discussions with immigration attorneys, if we expand into that area, we will likely have to lease an office or at least have access for our clients to meet with attorneys. Overall, in order to satisfy clients' needs, the virtual law firm may need to have some in-person options.

More on subscription business plans

The benefit of subscription legal services to small businesses is affordable, on call assistance to common legal issues; essentially for some it's fractional access to general counsel. The benefit to the law firm is that it improves cash flow, creates recurring revenue, and allows the lawyers to establish a more proactive relationship with the client to prevent many serious legal issues.

SLG will also use its website to improve delivery of legal services and increase affordability, including subscription plans that include simple transactional services (e.g., prenuptial agreements, NDAs, etc.) that can be purchased online. Many of these transactional services will be semi-automated and all attorney-reviewed for relevance and accuracy before being delivered to the client. By automating a large part of the workflow, SLG will be able to service more clients more affordably than a traditional legal practice.

In conclusion, when reflecting on how much has changed, or not, since the pandemic started, as I open SLG it appears that the answer must be, not much. All eyes are on Arizona with just three ABS firms approved in the first eight months of the program, all law firms. With SLG we applied to be a traditional firm that also offers mediation and collaborative law services; the former may be delivered by non-lawyers. Other states have set up committees to explore these models and law firms should keep an eye on this new model. With the ability for non-lawyers to invest and direct law firms, the competition for clients will increase and the ABS firms may have an advantage.

However, the goals and performance metrics remain the same for all law firms, whether ABS or not. Measurements must include client-facing KPIs because billable hour and profits per partner are not enough to ensure success. Using client satisfaction metrics and measuring firm culture are important, regardless of industry. A commitment to educate rather than sell and also to delight clients by providing simple, affordable, timely legal services predates the pandemic.

References

1. Disclaimer: the word non-lawyer is only being used because it's descriptive and easier than writing "other than lawyers" each time.

2. www.singular.law
3. www.azcourts.gov/Licensing-Regulation/Alternative-Business-Structure/How-to-apply-for-ABS-licensure. The Arizona Code of Judicial Administration section 7-209 sets forth the regulatory and licensing structure for ABSs, effective 1 January 2021. The requirements of the ABS application process appear in Code section 7-209(E) and (G)(1).
4. www.azcourts.gov/Licensing-Regulation/Alternative-Business-Structure/How-to-apply-for-ABS-licensure. Last visited 26 July 2021.
5. www.pewresearch.org/hispanic/fact-sheet/latinos-in-the-2016-election-arizona/.
6. www.cdc.gov/visionhealth/basics/ced/fastfacts.htm#.

Chapter 7: The value of non-legal skills in the management of law firms

By Jon Whittle, Jon Whittle Consulting Ltd

As we emerge from the pandemic, many law firms will underestimate the importance of commercial skills in the new normal that will develop. More concerning is that many law firms will assume that they can maintain their businesses, on their own, relying on the legal talent that worked before – a decision that could lead them disastrously astray.

Law firms that incorporate experience from the commercial world into driving their business forward can and will win in surprising ways. Similarly, adding experienced commercial voices into management teams will help firms find routes forward that avoid the pitfalls of going back to the old ways, whilst exploiting the new opportunities of the post-pandemic deregulated world.

In this chapter I will explain why sound commercial strategy is going to be as important as legal talent in the post-pandemic world and talk about why non-legal skills need to sit as equal voices in the management of law firms going forward. Now, more than ever, being a good lawyer is definitely not enough to run a good law firm. Good law firms need, first and foremost, to be good, fully rounded commercial businesses. Those that confuse being a good law firm with being a good business will struggle to survive in the cold, commercially astute world of post-pandemic legal services.

I challenge law firms to test that they can harness the power of non-legal business skills to advance the aims of their business. Can they build a business plan for their law firm that recognizes and properly utilizes non-legal business skills to drive their firm forward?

Why is there a problem?

For generations, law firms have been owned and run by lawyers and law firms have, largely, existed in a world where the only significant competition has been other law firms. Regulation has also gone out of its way to prevent legal services being sold by entities who are not owned and run by lawyers.

For many law firms, the quality of their legal offering is all that matters – being able to provide "good law" drives all other considerations before it. Most law firms obsess about their legal offering without fully appreciating how little this can resonate with the majority of their clients. Many fail to fully appreciate that clients will assume that the legal service they are buying will be "good law".

What clients *actually* want from their law firm is a legal service that is fit for their purpose, that suits their own needs and addresses their own objectives.

Law firms need to confront the central challenge that undermines their traditional business model. Most law firms massively overestimate how good they are, whilst massively underestimating how poorly they are perceived by their clients.

There are statistics to support these assertions, from a wide-ranging market research survey I conducted for LexisNexis a couple of years ago. Lawyers are three times more likely to think they provide good value than their clients (76 percent of lawyers rate the value of the service they provide as either excellent or very good, whilst the comparable figure for their clients is 27 percent). Similarly, three-quarters of lawyers think they are very good or excellent at customer service, whilst over a third of clients rate legal customer service as poor or, at best, average.[1]

Misunderstanding the value journey of clients leaves traditional law firms massively exposed to competitors for whom client value has always been the central part of their offering. The firm that values the client's output as much, if not more, than their own legal input is the firm that will win.

The traditionally regulated law firm is now entering a deregulated market where suppliers, who understand the demands of the client, will win. Thanks to the pandemic, many of the drivers of change are accelerating faster than ever before and deregulated, customer-focused, businesses will quickly usurp law firms relying on traditional management structures and an out-of-date service ethos.

Why commercial skills matter now

Most commentators agree that the UK legal market is heading into a period of unprecedented adjustment. The pandemic may have pushed back the impact of many of the forces of change, but they are still there and they will be just as disruptive as previously forecast. For many firms, the post-pandemic world is going to be an increasingly challenging space and those firms that fall back on their pre-pandemic working practices and plans will struggle to survive, let alone thrive.

I can think of no other commercial market, operating at a national and global level, that has been able to grow so big and to be so successful without having to deal with the normal pressures of open market competition. It is not, therefore, particularly surprising to discover that the legal world, as an industry, invests relatively little intellectual or commercial capital in areas such as sales, marketing, or customer service – processes that are usually at the core of every business.

In a competitive post-pandemic world, law firms will absolutely need authentic commercial skills built into the heart of their operations and be adept at putting these disciplines at the center of their business planning. A properly developed commercial strategy will be crucial if firms are to thrive. As the market starts to rid itself of the protections traditional law firms have previously enjoyed, a new generation of clients (and employees) will look for law firms that do business in ways that suit their way of living.

The post-pandemic law firm is going to have to compete in ways many will have never experienced before:

- Firms will have to adapt their service delivery to meet new clients and new client expectations. The demand for user-friendly services, delivered in ways that fit their clients' own circumstances, will increase exponentially;
- Firms will have to adapt their employment models to remain attractive to a changing legal workforce. A generation of lawyers with radically different expectations will be attracted to firms who understand and support their career aspirations;
- Law firms are going to have to learn to compete with non-legal businesses who can now employ lawyers and sell legal services (aside from the six reserved legal activities);
- Firms will have to learn how to compete with a new generation of independent consultant solicitors who can now work and sell their services outside the constraints of a regulated law firm;
- Firms that do not embrace and deploy the power of technology will find themselves attempting to deliver a legal service that no longer meshes, seamlessly, into the worlds of their clients and the businesses that employ them; and
- The pressure from clients on charges will ramp up substantially with a concomitant downward pressure on law firm revenues. Competition from legal services that operate using entirely different cost and

charging structures will threaten the financial model on which many law firms have relied for generations.

In addition to this long list of change, the costs of running a traditional, regulated firm will continue to increase, putting pressure on overheads and margins. Law firms that do not adapt and prepare for the changes coming in the post-pandemic world will struggle. Firms that prepare and remain agile and commercial and that make their businesses fit-for-purpose have the opportunity to develop radically.

What does "normal" look like?

In a conventional, non-legal, business it is expected (or even assumed) that the management team will be built around a wide range of complementary skills. It is also assumed that the entity will have a business plan, a strategy and a five- to ten-year operating plan. Alongside executive and operating officers, one would expect senior specialists in finance, HR, marketing, customer service, sales, product, and technology. The management team work together to pull each of these levers. All involved, by definition, completely recognize that the whole is greater than the sum of the parts.

Most of the above does not apply to the majority of law firms. I would contend, however, that these things should be built into every law firm of any scale at all. Even smaller firms should be ensuring that they have a business and operating plan and the resources on board to deliver both.

Law firms, owned and run by lawyers, are running the risk of being left behind in the new world order. Most law firms have, of course, incorporated non-legal skills into their operations and it is now not uncommon to find marketing, IT, HR, finance, and administration specialists working within law firms. The challenge is when these skills are not built into the DNA of the enterprise and when law firms lack the will to use these skills effectively. In almost all circumstances the balance of power, the decision-making heart of a legal organization, still rests, exclusively, in the hands of a management team composed of lawyers. This means that decisions about strategy, about commercial direction, about how the firm sets itself up and goes to market, are often taken in an environment where non-legal skills are not just absent but regarded as essentially irrelevant.

The legal advice that law firms provide is always only ever one part of the broader commercial mix of their commercial business offering. The legal talent and the services they deliver should not dictate the business plan, nor should it dictate how that plan is delivered. In the overwhelming majority of law firms, the role that non-legal talent – marketing, sales, customer service, technology – can play in the delivery of a commercially successful growth strategy is frequently misunderstood and often hugely neglected.

The only meaningful way to deliver a good business plan is to focus on all aspects of the business offering. If a law firm can pull the levers of marketing, sales, and customer service *effectively* then it can compete with non-legal providers for whom these disciplines are already a core component of their business set-up.

In order to do this, a law firm must focus on acquiring, nurturing, and valuing non-legal commercial skills.

What should law firms do to make themselves fit for the post-pandemic market?

It is not surprising that legal clients find law firms so challenging to work with.

In an environment where most law firms essentially deliver the same client benefits, regardless of supplier, it becomes ever more important for marketing and sales functions to drive individual firms to prominence.

To stand out, therefore, requires a proactive approach to marketing and sales – one that is designed to attract and retain the target customer. An approach that recognizes their vital importance and does not treat them as subservient to the legal services offered by the firm.

It is important to recognize that effective marketing and sales in law firms does not require specialist legal knowledge or an intimate understanding of the law. For the majority of law firms, marketing and selling legal services require, first and foremost, an understanding of the potential client and an ability to talk, using the client's language, about how the firm can address their needs and requirements.

It all starts with a good business plan. As discussed, law firms tend to focus on the development of their product (legal services) but often pay lip service to areas such as market positioning, sales, marketing, and other, essential, commercial levers.

Starting from first principles and building a business plan can help law firms structure their operations in a way that gives appropriate value to each of the commercial drivers. A good mission statement is the sum of the parts of a good business plan, which draws together all the elements that determine why the business can succeed. I would contend that many law firms need to invest more energy, time, and resource incorporating the non-legal elements of a successful business plan into their operations.

A law firm should be saying something about their business that is unique to them, that defines who they are and what they do. If a law firm's mission statement could belong, equally, to any one of ten other law firms, then how can a prospective client possibly choose and how does the firm know where to invest or how to build a strategy for growth? Equally, how would they defend themselves from competitor attack?

In a world of rapidly increasing choice, legal market deregulation, and growing client power, it is vital that law firms have a clear understanding of where they sit in the market. They need to know where opportunity lies and where threat exists. They must have a clear understanding of their strengths (and these need to be defined in relation to the market) and where there might be weakness in their total offering. If a law firm has not tested their business against these metrics, then they are exposed. Significantly, it is important that the firm tests all aspects of their operation against these metrics. All too often, firms measure their strength and their weaknesses purely, or even exclusively, on their own perception of the quality of their legal work. In essence, they only look at the product and neglect to think about the market in which they operate and what their competitors are doing. They also often neglect to look at non-legal providers of legal services as competition. Again, being able to take a holistic view of the market requires a view that embraces a wider perspective than that of the legal talent.

The balance of the complementary legal and commercial skills should be determined by the nature of the firm. The firm needs to know what sort of business they are running and structure their management and operations accordingly.

Next steps on the journey to commercial success

Strategy first, structure second. Start from first principles and know what your business is for, why it exists, where it is going, and what success will look like. Every employee in your firm should absolutely know what their firm will be like if they all "win" – otherwise how can they do their job?

Building a successful business strategy is not difficult but it can be hard to achieve if done in a vacuum or without external input. A law firm without a robust strategy runs the risk of building ad hoc structures or simply evolves, organically, without having a clear plan for how the various departments, divisions and processes work together towards a common, clearly identified goal.

The most powerful tool, in my experience, is to break down the walls that surround the legal management team. Often the simplest way to start the process is to look outside the legal profession for help. Bringing in a non-exec, either permanently or on a project basis to sit with the senior leadership and help build a commercial plan for the law firm is a powerful lever to driving change.

A good non-exec can drive change rapidly and effectively – but all firms should test that they can deliver the following checklist, and deliver it from a commercial perspective, not a law firm perspective.

- Define your market. Who are your future clients? Where are they and what do they want?
- Focus on client needs. Starting from first principles to define what good service looks like – but *entirely* from the client's perspective.
- Define your point of difference. What sets your firm apart – what makes it special? Is it defendable? Does your client understand?
- Determine the skills you need and how to harness output to support strategy. Identify the resources and skills and build internal structures to ensure that these resources are used effectively.

The future for law firms is exciting – legal services are on the cusp of fundamental change and the market is expanding rather than contracting. In the rapidly changing world order, the successful law firms will be the ones who put service first and build their businesses around helping clients get what they want and need. There are many rapidly moving parts involved in getting this done well but the prize is worth the effort.

References

1. The LexisNexis Bellwether Report 2016, The Riddle of Perception. LexisNexis UK Ltd: www.lexisnexis.co.uk/bellwether/reports.html.

Chapter 8:
Dispute resolution from A to Z – will remote practice prevail?

By Mary Juetten, Traklight

Like many other lawyers, I embraced remote work for meetings, trainings, and client interactions as we made our way through 2020 and into mid-2021. Now emerging into a post-pandemic world, the question is whether our legal system, including all means of dispute resolution – courts and beyond – will continue to serve people with fully remote systems.

Research shows that only about three percent of all civil matters go to court in the United States,[1] which means that the "alternative" dispute resolution (ADR) avenues dominate and actually are the norm, not the exception. Within the field, there is also the early dispute resolution model, which may include training to prevent conflict or, at a minimum, planned interventions to avoid even the threat of litigation. During the pandemic, ZDR (Zoom Dispute Resolution) became the de-facto means for court proceedings, mediation, meetings, training, education, bar exams, and more. Several technologies were launched or relaunched, including augmented or artificial intelligence (AI) for disputes. This chapter explores the impact and staying power of remote dispute resolution and AI on the role of lawyers and legal training.

Why "alternative"?

First a word on the letter A in the ADR moniker or acronym. The American Bar Association (ABA) is organized by practice type and separates its litigation section from the newly titled Dispute Resolution (DR) section. In my home state of Washington, the non-litigation group is still called the ADR section, like many other state legal groups. As only a small percentage of civil litigation matters end up in court, it seems that DR is the correct term for the lion's share of legal disputes. However, when the ABA's DR website is reviewed, the term ADR comes up repeatedly. Although this may seem like just semantics, it's important in several ways for the general public and small businesses.

First, when people in the US are wronged, they immediately think lawsuit. The average US citizen does not understand the high likelihood of using another means to resolve the dispute. How many times have you purchased a product or registered for a service and actually signed away your right to litigate? More than you would know, because truth be told, most of us do not read the fine print nor the click-through online terms of service. For example, American mobile phone agreements stipulate that you cannot litigate and some call for binding arbitration as the sole dispute resolution method.

Second, even pre-pandemic, the time for a matter to crawl through the US court system is measured in years, not months. As civil courts stop remote sessions and return to in-person, any efficiencies will be lost and the pace will likely be negatively impacted. Also, with the large number of pent-up disputes such as evictions, bankruptcies, and the explosion of family law matters, the system will be slower than ever.

Finally, the cost of litigation in areas outside of the large cities is beyond the average person's or company's budget, even before going to an actual trial. The pandemic did not reduce lawyer hourly rates and, in the civil areas mentioned above, lawyers are now in high demand, which may see increases in costs for clients.

All of the above appears to signal that it is a mistake to fully return to in-person and lose some of the efficiencies of remote courts for lawyers and clients alike. Some courts and agencies have held telephonic conferences and trials for years. However, unfortunately, the US legal system does not revolve around clients' needs, nor is there any appetite for a complete overhaul to move court completely online. Instead, the move appears to be back to more of the same.

Preventative dispute resolution

Let's take a step back to look at the pre-litigation phase of dispute resolution, because conflict is an inevitable part of life and of business. Despite the unavoidable nature of conflict, we often attempt to avoid issues and some go to great lengths to hide from potential disputes. There is an early dispute resolution (EDR) school of thought that believes that quick intervention in conflicts can head off the involvement of lawyers, remote or otherwise. In other words, a way to broaden the word "alternative" in ADR is to insert non-legal assistance early within the continuum of a dispute and to also provide education to those who work in high conflict areas.

A recent example is a large technology manufacturer in the US that created a program for its construction project managers and commercial team to train, along with contractors, on early detection and resolution of potential issues. Rather than creating and driving a conflict environment from day one with escalating exchanges of contract letters, instead there is a process for sharing information, openly discussing conflict, thus preserving relationships while moving forward. Inserting such a process into company culture, with appropriate training, means not only less litigation but also on-time and on-budget projects.

These programs and conflict resolution strategies are not limited to the in-house legal team but instead include project managers, finance, and commercial personnel, and on-the-ground supervisors. When the interests of the owner, engineering firms, and the construction companies are recognized and aligned, legal disputes can be avoided.

Technology and artificial intelligence (AI)

With respect to smaller scale disputes, there are online platforms in many countries that address consumer conflicts around e-commerce with automation or "expert systems", including bot technology. While the individual transaction amounts are not large, the companies themselves are massive; small claims courts would come to a standstill if every PayPal, Amazon, or Etsy dispute were brought forward. Several platforms simply collect basic information and immediately transfer that dispute data to a live customer service person who will negotiate on behalf of the company. Other companies have systems to receive monetary offers to settle from both sides online and use algorithms to work out a solution, all without human intervention.

Unfortunately, a simple blind bidding system that works to address small monetary disputes is still considered taking work away from lawyers and mediators rather than a sound use of technology to improve access to conflict resolution. Further, while these platforms are not true AI but more like augmented intelligence, the reaction by many legal professionals has been negative. When the average American cannot receive a timely day in court and in most states almost 80 percent of citizens cannot access legal support, this level of protectionism is unwarranted.[2]

True artificial intelligence (AI), systems, and technology that involve interpreting speech patterns, facial emotions and more tend to be viewed with suspicion by lawyers. Although some of this technology is still beyond current capabilities, the overwhelming amount of dispute resolution work cries out for technological assistance. It's an important distinction to refer to AI as assisting the process, rather than completely replacing the human. This assistance can be provided remotely but in addition to, and just as importantly, within the conference or courtroom where the parties are meeting.

In my former career as a professional accountant, I embraced early technology that moved my work from messy and difficult to balance handwritten worksheets to electronic spreadsheets with automatic totals. As a mediator, if technology can be used to enhance the practice of resolving disputes, I welcome that innovation.

Mediation

When I took my mediation training during the early days of the pandemic, it was exclusively online, including the simulated sessions where we worked through disputes. This approach is not new; my Masters in Law was almost all online coursework and I have taught law school classes using various distance learning platforms for several years. Again, with the current and increasing backlog of cases, training on all aspects of dispute resolution must remain readily available. More on this below.

Over the past 18 months, I have spoken with numerous experienced mediators who have conducted all their work using Zoom for years prior to the pandemic. Many cite reasons around clients' needs, including safety and convenience. Some have exclusively used text or asynchronous messaging to work with clients on their own time and at their own pace. One lawyer has mediated over 500 court cases using the chat function on a mediation case management platform – no Zoom or other video technology, only text-like communications. There are several companies that have created systems for courts to funnel cases for mediation and have both synchronous and asynchronous communication capability.

One key concern is the confidentiality of the mediation process. Obviously, it's easy to maintain when the parties are in the same room. Zoom and other remote collaboration technologies struggled initially with security issues around access but, at this point, there are means to ensure that the sessions are secure, including the private caucuses within one larger meeting. However, the idea that non-parties may be sitting off-camera or in another room within hearing distance remains very possible. This level of dishonesty by some does not mean that mediation should return to in-person for all.

In addition, I have heard that blind-bidding or bot-assisted mediation may be construed to remove the self-determination aspect of the mediation process. For example, looking to the consumer participant as a small claim versus a family law party, this notion of preserving the human-only interaction is not necessary to resolve a likely pure monetary transaction.

However, in the family law setting, the future relationship can be important, particularly if there are children involved. In that case, the use of technology should be tailored to the specifics of the situation.

Collaborative law

Another broadening of conflict resolution service providers beyond just lawyers is the use of a collaborative law team rather than only attorneys. The collaborative law approach started in family law and initially involved two lawyers who would proceed to resolve the case using interest-based negotiation. Now expanded to include other civil matters, collaborative law generally involves a lawyer for each party but instead of experts on each side, such as financial support professionals (including business valuators) and mental health professionals, there is only one of each type of expert involved. Many states have legislation that allows parties to stay the litigation process during the civil collaborative law process if a case has already been filed. The focus of collaborative law is on the relationships and a resolution that allows for both a solution and a path forward.

As the collaborative law movement grows beyond family law into estate planning, small business, and construction matters, teams can use ZDR for productive meetings instead of bringing everyone together in one room. However, as the world opens up, there may be a tendency to default back to in-person meetings. Ultimately, like the rest of the legal services, the clients' needs and desires should dictate the meetings in terms of whether they are online or in person.

Online education

If the public can resolve disputes with technology, including the use of augmented and eventually artificial intelligence, what does that mean for education for the professionals that support the process? During the pandemic, many courses and conferences were postponed or cancelled. However, several in-person providers instead shifted to online courses.

At a minimum, dispute professionals, including lawyers, should understand and be comfortable with the use of technology to enhance their practice, both within the room and in delivery outside their four walls. Learning in the same manner as the service will be delivered is beneficial to those who are not comfortable working remotely. For example, my mediation course was completely online, including all the simulations. This prepared me for ZDR better than any in-person class. The same can be said of my collaborative law trainings, again all done online.

Most law schools went quickly to remote learning and it was reported as not very successful for the majority of students. Thinking back to my own in-person law school experience, I can see why it would not work as well online. However, the solution may not be to go back to in-person but perhaps revisit the materials and methodology. We may have missed the time to shift law school learning to become more practical and less Socratic. Yet, as we come back to in-person learning, it appears that nothing will change for the law school experience, nor the bar exams. Unfortunately, the pandemic was only a brief reprieve and now it's Big Law business as usual at most schools.

Small steps forward

During the pandemic, we were thrown into the proverbial deep end and had to go fully remote to keep our legal systems functioning, albeit in many cases in a reduced fashion. Now that we are returning to some type of normalcy, it's disheartening to see that those who plan to continue to practice virtually are still considered unusual. I belong to several groups and it's clear that the notion of permanent remote work remains a novelty.

My hope is that we do not jump back to 100 percent in-person work. That is not just because I wish to stay on Zoom in my business casual clothing from the waist up and my comfortable exercise pants, but rather because of my clients' feedback. My current mediation work is all undertaken online or over the phone and this has provided more access for clients. My area of practice is commercial real estate matters and my clients include landlords and tenants alike, all with a variety of work hours. I can meet their schedules and, as many run businesses, the traditional work hours do not fit their needs. There is no need to schedule extra travel time to meet with me at an office nor worry about a conversation being too short for a meeting.

The needs of both clients and professionals in individual areas of dispute resolution must be addressed but the weight should be towards the client, which is not always the case with legal services. These dispute resolution services should be assessed and the impact of returning to in-person carefully measured from the clients' perspective. Beyond actual interactions with clients, there is a requirement to ensure that all systems support remote attendance. For example, meetings and conferences that were solely remote should continue to have an option for people to join from other places, even when they move back to in-person. It should be noted that the level of participation may drop if we move to solely in-person, particularly for state-wide or national organizations. This means that technology-sharing tools beyond just an online video platform should support these events and collaboration amongst all.

In addition, the court systems need to support online participation, because not all clients (or lawyers for that matter) are located in large cities near courts. One example is the adoption of online state-wide filings that facilitate attorneys' representation of clients.

Beyond ZDR

Automating a bad practice or adding technology to a faulty process does not improve the system to resolve disputes and, in turn, does not increase access to justice. In addition, a sub-standard lawyer or mediator will not perform better doing ZDR or using technology. An analysis and optimization of the professional's dispute resolution workflow will generate the ideas necessary for enhancement.

How do we go beyond just Zoom and other remote connection platforms? We start at the beginning and provide education and information online for those potential clients who are searching for help with their disputes. A basic understanding of clients' needs will allow for the development of technology and tools that can augment dispute resolution. Whether it's a virtual intake checklist, a bot that answers frequently asked questions, an online risk assessment, or simple scheduling tools, the right technology will both enhance the professional's practice and improve the clients' experience.

Evaluating the staying power of remote

During the pandemic, almost all alternatives to litigation were online and most courts have functioned exclusively online. Although, in the US, criminal matters did drop, specifically drinking and driving infractions, there were still some in-person requirements but civil courts functioned mainly online. That said, there is an incredible pent-up demand associated with landlord–tenant, bankruptcy, and family law matters, which will further constrain our systems once the country opens up and the eviction moratoriums expire. Some states are examining mandatory mediation for all such civil matters to unburden the courts.

The question now becomes whether we can agree that "alternative" dispute resolution methods should be the avenue of first choice or the norm. Do lawyers have the mindset to find the best way for their clients to resolve differences without automatically resorting to litigation? Further, should the lawyers decide whether that ADR approach is online or in-person? Should it truly be the managing partners' edict to drive a return to the office for a fixed number of days a week as we have recently seen in the news? Or should clients' needs drive the type and location of dispute resolution support provided, regardless of whether a lawyer is involved?

Luckily, the future of dispute resolution does not solely rely upon the legal profession. As a start, mediators do not have to be qualified lawyers in the US. Alternatives to attorneys are growing; the state of Arizona passed legislation in late 2020 that allows for a non-lawyer legal practitioner (LP) in various areas, including family and business law. Unlike some states' approach to paraprofessionals' certifications, the LP will be able to represent clients in court on a limited scope basis. In addition, Arizona has become the first state to allow non-lawyers to invest in or own a law firm with annual renewals. The state's Alternative Business Structure (ABS) legislation passed last fall and already three firms are approved to operate. These ABS firms are not part of a trial sandbox approach like some other states.

Allowing additional ownership and investment will hopefully also bring more of a business- and client-centered focus to the law, particularly with respect to resolving disputes. Whether it's an early intervention or conflict process after a lawsuit is filed, creating alternatives for clients that permanently include online options will improve access to justice.

References

1. https://bjs.ojp.gov/content/pub/pdf/cbjtsc05.pdf.
2. www.lsc.gov/about-lsc/what-legal-aid/unmet-need-legal-aid.

Chapter 9: Consolidation in a post-pandemic legal sector

By Viv Williams, Viv Williams Consulting

Most of the 10,400 legal practices in the UK had a "good pandemic" and dealt with the challenges by using government support well. Many firms were financially stronger in 2021 than they were going into lockdown in March 2020; turnover was down but so were costs, so furloughing and funding meant that firms had cash in the bank. However, we cannot ignore the challenges facing the profession, and the pandemic has sped up the eventuality of consolidation.

Let's explore how other professions have changed. There used to be independently owned opticians in every town and city across the UK, but gradually these became unviable as the use of technology and the growth of corporations such as Vision Express and Specsavers took hold, with a more corporate structure led by volume purchasing. There are now very few independent opticians left in the UK.

The veterinary profession is on the same journey, with private equity-backed corporates purchasing and consolidating the independent vets' practice. In fact, the desire to build brand awareness has resulted in the growth of vets being attached to pet supermarkets. The race to scale these businesses has seen extraordinary premiums being paid to acquire local vets' practices – the EBITDA of these practices has risen to as high as 20 for a chain of practices in multiple locations.

The legal profession has just started on this journey with a few private equity houses supporting the consolidator firms, providing the necessary capital to grow by acquiring other firms with specific disciplines. We have seen a growing number of flotations on the various stock markets and an appetite from institutions to support this trend, with many more planning this route. As we will explore in this chapter, there are a number of reasons why this trend will continue, with the pandemic simply bringing it forward. We will see large numbers of firms question their future strategy, with numerous acquirers willing to purchase most types of practices or, at the very least, their clients and books of business.

Structural change

Back in 2007, the Law Society was the representative body and regulator of the legal profession, and many traditional aspects had remained the same for many years. For example, a solicitor's practice had to be a partnership or an LLP, and it was only following the launch of the Solicitors Regulation Authority (SRA) in 2007 that we began to experience changing structures and new initiatives. Some 14 years later, according to this organization, we now have approximately 70 percent of legal firms operating as limited liability companies and increasingly being subject to company law. We have also seen the growth of the Alternative Business Structure (ABS), which allows non-lawyers to own solicitors' practices. This is a double-edged sword for the profession. On one side we have the growth and investment from private equity houses taking ownership of firms, which gives law firms the cash they need for growth and acquisitions. On the other side, it gives the opportunity to others to enter the profession, such as accountants, insurance companies, and IFAs, who can employ solicitors to deliver legal work without the cost of compliance and regulation.

In March 2020 we faced the issue of aging owners and dwindling profits, with more than 3,000 firms still operating under traditional partnership or LLP models but all operating in a partnership way; in other words, drawing all the profits and not retaining any profit in the business itself. As we return to some degree of normality, these issues haven't changed and we are beginning to see a significant growth in merger activity. Many smaller firms are seeking merger partners, but sadly many of these are unattractive to potential buyers and their only solution seems to be controlled closure. The cost of this would be devastating for the current owners who had spent 30 years building a business that no one wants.

Succession crisis

There is no doubt that we are facing a succession crisis within the legal profession with many firms not given adequate time to plan their exit. The average age of a law firm owner is 65 years. Few have faced the succession issue, hoping it will all just go away. There are numerous examples of firms that have thought that associates and younger salaried partners would jump at the chance to become an owner in their profitable firm. Many of these have resulted in the offer of ownership being declined and the current owners (usually in their sixties) left with a dilemma. I recently visited a firm where the above had happened. Two equity partners in their late fifties had incorporated from an LLP to a limited company in 2019 but the younger potential owners did not want the responsibility of ownership and the risk that it entails. This left them with a serious issue – rather than planning their exit through succession they are now considering selling the practice. A healthy profitable business in a high-net-worth area should be attractive to a prospective acquirer but what they thought was a plan has now turned into something else. This type of scenario is happening all over the country with profitable businesses finding it difficult to plan their exit successfully.

Utilizing a non-executive director

Many law firms, whatever their size or structure, are utilizing the skills of a non-executive director (NED) as part of their management. With interest from both private equity and the numbers of floated law firms and planned flotations, it sometimes becomes an enforced necessity to have a NED on the management board. With over 70 percent of law firms now limited liability companies, the role of the NED can be an invaluable asset to all law firms. The remaining 30 percent can still take advantage of a virtual NED to guide them through the change management process that all firms need.

The banks are looking very cynically at the way many professional practices are operated and traditional bank funding by overdraft and loans will change dramatically over the next decade. Most partners/directors of law firms have grown up with traditional bank lending and find it difficult to understand alternative funding in the future – the NED will understand how this works and guide the business along the right path.

We are all aware of the challenges facing the legal profession, but these legislative, fiscal and succession issues can be eased by having a NED or virtual NED on board. Decisions that are made by partners, who are often ill equipped or experienced in managing change, can be challenged by someone who is not involved in the day-to-day running of a busy practice. Business skills can be brought into play, making individual departments more profitable, constantly reviewing working processes and finding new and unusual ways of running a law firm as a business.

Most NEDs or virtual NEDs will improve the law firm's profitability considerably and help avoid many of the pitfalls that partners can find themselves within. The role will bring a different dimension to law firm management and those firms who have willingly embraced the role have found the advantages far outweigh the cost. The cost of the NED will vary depending on the size of the practice, the time required, and the disciplines involved, but would not exceed the day rate of your normal hourly charge.

Many banks now encourage a non-exec presence within law firm management, recognizing the value of a non-lawyer helping with the vision and strategy, and someone with business acumen reviewing the management of a law firm with non-lawyer eyes. It's easy to become isolated within a legal practice and the focus becomes very internal – "working in the practice and not on it". A NED or virtual NED can also find ways of reviewing the working capital requirements of a practice. Law firm funding and traditional overdrafts and loans will become the exception rather than the norm. Finding the essential alternative – a type of invoice discounting – will become more commonplace, and the NED should be able to provide sufficient knowledge and guidance in the right circumstances.

Professional indemnity premiums

For the past 20 years we have experienced a soft insurance market, and some would argue that we have become complacent, with new insurers wanting to buy premiums each year. However, this is no longer the case with some insurers not taking on new business. We have seen a gradual and progressive rise in claims outweighing the size of premiums in the past few years and following disasters such as Grenfell, insurers are wary about mounting claims. The legal profession, just like other sectors, has been forced into home working and this, dependent on the robustness of their IT systems, has left many insurers nervous about what impact the lack of supervision of staff could have on future claims. The conveyancing market has been incredibly busy following the stamp duty holiday and without excellent IT, home working could well exacerbate a rise in claims. This, coupled with a hardening insurance market, has seen professional indemnity premiums rise dramatically in the last two years.

A 30 percent increase in an annual premium was affordable, particularly when CIBLS and BBLS were available to fund premiums. If the conveyancing turnover of a law firm is in excess of 25 percent of the turnover, then the average premium has risen by 30 percent year-on-year. However, this is subject to a good claims history. For those firms with multiple claims, some insurers have simply refused to quote, even for existing policy holders. There are exceptions and some firms have seen a premium increase quadruple over two years. With no Government funding, will premiums be affordable in the coming years, and will this drive more firms to look for a merger?

Conveyancing staff have been increasingly difficult to find throughout the pandemic and some firms have not only substantially increased the fees they charge but turned work away. Many law firm owners have found the pressure to keep clients informed and happy hard to withstand, and have worked impossible hours during the pandemic. Many are now saying they have gone as far as they can with their firm and are looking to merge or sell. Is this a catalyst for greater consolidation?

Even specialist conveyancers have found the insurance market difficult to navigate with several CLC regulated firms unable to obtain insurance. What was once the bedrock and solid cash generator for many practices has become a real challenge for those firms without the resources to deliver and could force a number of firms to stop offering conveyancing to their clients. Without affordable professional indemnity insurance, how many firms will be forced into merger talks?

Market disruption

We have discussed how the change in regulator back in 2007 has impacted on the profession with the growth of new models to disrupt the traditional legal sector. Weak management and outdated operating models have been partially responsible for this much-needed change and the death knell for the High Street practice that is here to stay.

Although not new, the growth in firms operating in the solicitor consultant model has been meteoric through the pandemic, with many individual solicitors choosing to change the way they work. Traditional firms without the necessary investment in IT have forced solicitors to come into an office to work and many have realized that a self-employed consultancy role suits their work–life balance much better.

The consultant model works on the "eat what you kill" premise, so having a good number of existing clients is an essential ingredient to the individual solicitor's success. Those solicitors that have been "fed" work by the marketing departments of their firm find it difficult to become a marketing machine and tend to be less successful, but for an individual with a good client following, it can be very lucrative, with income splits ranging from 60/40 to 80/20, with the law firm taking the majority of the risk. In some cases, it may be an exit route for firms to become a virtual franchise with the firm paying the PI premium and the majority of the administration costs – yet they still receive 70 percent of their income.

The growth in the number of firms offering this type of model has come at a price; the investment they have made in technology has been high and although somewhat prescriptive seems to satisfy both investors and insurers alike in the success of the model.

The pandemic has accelerated the need to become "officeless" and investment in infrastructure, reduced support staff, and cost efficiency has given many of these firms a considerable advantage over the traditional practice. Consumers seem more comfortable in purchasing legal services remotely and this can only be seen as true market disruption.

This sets another challenge to traditional law firms that, without government financial support, are reluctant to make significant owner investment into cost reduction and technology. This will mean that the "squeezed middle" will be traditional firms, mainly regional, which will find it increasingly difficult to compete on price.

As discussed earlier, many solicitors do not want the responsibility of ownership and many will find it attractive to be part of a bigger firm as a consultant with a better work–life balance, and possibly a better income.

Cost efficiency

Many legal services are technology- and process-driven and the efficient firm will look towards investment in artificial intelligence (AI). Outsourcing and offshoring will become an effective way of driving down costs and improving efficiency.

Consumers are becoming more comfortable in purchasing legal services through apps, and by using AI we will see a reduction in the full-time job market for solicitors. Anything that can be processed will be; from conveyancing to probate the world of legal services is changing beyond recognition. Bizarrely, the pandemic has sped up the need to process and a significant investment in technology is a step too far for many firms.

We have seen a significant growth in firms prepared to become more efficient by outsourcing and offshoring processed services. We have seen progressive firms reducing costs by around 40 percent by offshoring the file-opening and post-completion part of the conveyancing process. Utilizing this type of service has allowed firms to develop and grow and focus on more technical matters, and in fact I have seen firms doubling in size by adopting this efficient and cost-effective part of the process.

This will mean that more and more firms will not be able to compete in a highly competitive market and we will see a growth in the factory-type legal process centers already making a huge impact on smaller and mid-sized practices.

Consumer choice

The increase in "Trip Advisor" style websites is moving consumers towards less localized purchasing of legal services. These review websites give consumers the opportunity to base their choice of law firm upon other client experiences. Many practices have been guilty of poor client care over a number of years, and these websites encourage consumers to vote with their feet. This is another challenge to firms not prepared to change their way of working. Despite client loyalty, we are seeing a trend towards websites to purchase legal documents and templates primarily due to price.

Fundamentally, firms that are not providing exceptional client care will face a reduction in their turnover. Changing the culture of a practice is a slow and difficult process that takes both time and investment. I strongly suggest that many firms will gradually see their business diminish if this is not addressed.

The consolidators

For the first time to my knowledge, we currently have more acquirers of law firms than we have firms for sale. The demand to grow and acquire is currently outstripping the supply of firms for sale. This is due to the fact that most firms still have cash and are therefore not focused on their future direction. All the points highlighted in this chapter focus on the reasons why we will see consolidation and failures, but the majority of firms are at the crossroads in their decision-making and have not yet made the decision to merge.

Diminishing turnover and aging owners need a catalyst to help make their decisions for them, and as the professional indemnity season gets into full swing, this may be the point at which firms will look to merge. Certainly, over the next few years we will see a large number of mergers and potential failures.

The legal sector has always been fragmented and numerous small solicitor practices have built their reputation on word of mouth and local advertising. In many towns, solicitors have their offices on the same street, making it virtually impossible to compare one firm to another – a very similar situation to where opticians were several years ago.

We are now just starting to see national brands emerging, the first of which was Quality Solicitors, which operated as a type of franchise but had television advertising supporting the brand. Private equity has taken a significant interest in legal services and has supported numerous firms with their growth strategy. We have seen a number of these practices float on the various stock markets with institutional investment and there are many more to come.

A very different story is emerging, with smaller local firms unable to compete on volume processed services and therefore choosing to become more niche in their offering and dropping unprofitable or unviable lines of work. Others will join the merger mania and realize that they are unable to provide the services traditionally offered and need economies of scale to make their business profitable. Some will merge with local firms that eventually will be acquired by national corporate brands.

We have significant interest at all levels from private equity houses that see legal services as a lucrative space to be in. We have consolidators in the volume process arena such as conveyancing that have their own offshore captive that they process legal work through.

Other brands are emerging and becoming more nationally prominent as they continue to merge and acquire profitable practices. Perhaps this perfect storm will be the catalyst for change.

Chapter 10: Thriving in a post-pandemic world – cutting-edge law practice areas

By Sally Kane and Ashley B. Jordan, Reed Smith LLP

A new era of law practice

The COVID-19 pandemic has had a profound impact on the global legal landscape. Court backlogs, soaring litigation activity, shifting client priorities, and heightened security risks associated with greater technology adoption across industries will be among the factors that fuel demand for services across many legal sectors.

The pandemic has impacted virtually all segments of the legal profession, prompting a unique opportunity for firms and organizations to reimagine the practice of law.[1] As the world emerges from the grasp of COVID-19, the future promises to be busy and profitable for many law practice areas.

While litigation trends are developing, the full impact of the pandemic on law practice may take time to emerge. However, one thing is certain – the COVID-19 pandemic has left its mark on the world and forever changed law practice. Lawyers will continue to navigate unprecedented territory as they tackle novel obstacles and deliver legal services in the "new normal".

Several practice areas are poised for growth in the months and years following the pandemic – including insurance recovery, litigation, cyber law, labor and employment, private equity, regulatory and compliance, and health law. This chapter examines each in turn as well as the trends and forces fueling that growth.

Litigation

The COVID-19 pandemic is expected to generate more litigation than any other crisis in global history. As the world emerges from dark and troubled times, a surge in litigation activity across a broad range of industries has followed, including the particularly hard-hit transportation, energy, retail, travel, hospitality, manufacturing, education, recreational services, entertainment, and real estate industries.

The pandemic first prompted unprecedented and widespread courtroom shutdowns, primarily due to Coronavirus-related exposures and local government mandates. As those conditions have generally improved, the massive case backlog has been further impacted by a prioritized criminal docket. Notes Janet Kwuon, a litigation partner and co-chair of Reed Smith's global commercial disputes group, the legal industry is now also experiencing a flood of cases where the underlying dispute is related to pandemic-related issues, including challenges to government regulation regarding pandemic mandates, financial losses, personal injury and/or evictions.

Business interruption claims represent the highest number of lawsuits thus far as companies seek to recover losses arising from pandemic-related shutdowns, government-ordered closures and supply chain disruptions. According to legal analytics firm Lex Machina,[2] other practice areas experiencing a spike in COVID-related litigation include insurance, employment, contracts, securities, consumer protection, torts, civil rights, and trademark law.

Class actions are also gaining momentum in the United States, UK, continental Europe, Australia, and Canada as plaintiffs' lawyers and litigation funders seek to assist parties with their pandemic-related losses. Leading types of pandemic-related class actions include insurance, contract, employment, securities, and consumer protection claims.

Moving forward, law practice will be forever transformed by the pandemic. "The legal community has had to immediately and collectively transform itself. Even our most hardened Luddites are now facile with Zoom, Skype, Microsoft Teams and other similar platforms for hearings, depositions, mediations, and even trial," says Kwuon. "Counsel have had to become even more flexible and communicative with each other since many well-worn customs and practices have become impracticable, if not impossible. Going forward, the short-term increased efficiencies and cost savings related to remote proceedings will have to be balanced against the robust and substantive value of in-person interactions on all levels. Nevertheless, it is clear that the pandemic has created an additional pathway for managing disputes."

Insurance recovery

Every company is a policyholder. Insurance is the backbone of many industries; net premiums written by the United States' insurance industry totaled $1.28 trillion in 2020.[3]

When fortuitous events occur, policyholders turn to their insurance assets to provide bargained-for protection from losses. Given that insurance companies are built on a model that requires denial of claims to realize profit, insurance claim denials abound.

There are, naturally, spikes in the engagement of insurance recovery counsel after national or global scale events, such as the COVID-19 pandemic. To date, policyholders have engaged insurance recovery counsel to file more than 1,900 lawsuits against their carriers concerning coverage for COVID-19 business interruption losses. The need for insurance recovery counsel, however, remains constant given the insurance industry's business model.

"With the ongoing pandemic, supply chain challenges, and uptick in shareholder litigation and cyber liability claims, insurance recovery work is poised for exponential growth," says David Halbreich, a partner and chair of Reed Smith's insurance recovery group.

Post-pandemic, general counsel will continue to rely on insurance recovery counsel. Insurance policies tend to be labyrinths, and they are read in conjunction with governing case law, statutes, and regulations. Companies depend on insurance recovery counsel to help navigate the path forward, which is fraught with coverage pitfalls for even the largest, most sophisticated policyholders. Moreover, unlike many practices, insurance recovery functions as a cost recovery center for businesses. It is a profit-earning division, not simply an expense. Insurance recovery counsel gets claims and legal fees paid – and brings money into companies' legal departments.

Defense counsel will also seek out insurance recovery counsel to help coordinate defense and insurance goals – and avoid unforced errors that bear on coverage. In addition, insurance risk managers will lean on insurance recovery counsel to work with companies' insurance brokers to craft and negotiate "state-of-the-art" policies for businesses.

Insurance recovery counsel can assist companies in all aspects of the insurance recovery process:

- Counseling during the process of purchasing insurance policies;
- Analyzing insurance policies and facts surrounding a loss;
- Advising on the presentation of an insurance claim;
- Advising on securing forensic accounting and other expert support;
- Assuring compliance with statutory and insurance policy deadlines and post-loss obligations;
- Negotiation of partial payments;
- Documentary and witness assistance for claimed losses;
- Preparing a case to be successful if litigated; and
- Negotiating, mediating, arbitrating, or litigating an insurance claim as needed to maximize recovery.

The COVID-19 pandemic is a rapidly developing phenomenon. Hundreds of thousands of stateside businesses have careened into economic despair. With many businesses teetering, the need for insurance recovery counsel has never been greater. Businesses are and will continue to be in dire need for their insurance policies, across all lines of coverage, to respond to losses, pandemic-related or not. With this being a top priority as businesses seek to drive revenue post-pandemic, and absent disruption of the insurance industry model, insurance recovery counsel will remain in high demand for many years to come.

Cyber law

In the wake of the pandemic, organizations around the world face unprecedented security challenges. Hackers and cyber criminals are exploiting pandemic-related chaos, a remote workforce, and greater reliance on digital infrastructures as more businesses transfer business-critical functions to the cloud.

In the past year, the world has seen a wave of high-profile and large-scale attacks on financial institutions, health care organizations, essential services, law firms, retailers, and other organizations. Companies of all sizes and industries are seeing an uptick in phishing, ransomware, web application attacks, and a host of other cybersecurity issues.

The consequences of a cyberattack can be complex and costly, impacting an organization's reputation and bottom line. To combat the potential threat to their operations, organizations will rely on law firms to litigate a growing number of cyber claims and minimize exposure to cyberattacks, especially as such incidents grow more sophisticated and expensive. "In particular, organizations are incorporating ransomware mitigation components and planning in their incident response policies, and retaining legal counsel and forensics firms in advance of an attack to allow for an immediate and seamless reaction to an incident," says Sarah Bruno, a partner in Reed Smith's San Francisco office and a member of the firm's tech and data group. "Companies that are prepared do fare better."

In particular, to minimize vulnerabilities and liability, businesses will turn to law firms for help in bolstering their privacy and security practices, reevaluating their cybersecurity strategies and navigating potential cyber liability and risk management issues. Lawyers will also assist organizations in implementing cyber liability policies, controls, and procedures as part of an internal data privacy and network security incident response plan. This can be accomplished via workshops with the response team to update policies, confirm procedures, and conduct tabletop training exercises.

In the event of a loss, cyber liability insurance may be impacted. In the aftermath of the pandemic, clients will turn to insurance recovery lawyers for help in obtaining insurance recovery for claims, investigations, and losses arising from data and privacy security breaches, improper transmission, or disclosure of personal or proprietary data, ransomware attacks, and other growing cyber threats such as phishing and cryptojacking. Lawyers will also counsel clients in evaluating and negotiating cyber liability insurance policies and enhancements to maximize protection on all aspects of data privacy and network security.

"Not only are there costs that arise during the incident response, it is important to also consider the costs for cleaning it up," Bruno says. "There will be costs associated with remediation, server downtime, re-establishing the appropriate levels of security and equipment evaluation/replacement, as well as operational costs (and losses) as a result of the system downtime. Being proactive and having a plan could certainly help alleviate some of these costs, and it will also allow for organizations to negotiate better cyber insurance rates."

Labor and employment

The COVID-19 pandemic has ushered in a host of new workplace challenges that affect the employment landscape. Remote work is here to stay, and the health and safety of employees are at the forefront as employers navigate office re-openings and a hybrid workforce.

In the aftermath of the pandemic, organizations across the globe will seek guidance on COVID-19-related workplace issues, such as re-openings, compliance policies, leave of absence, and workplace safety. Employment law attorneys will also help clients establish post-pandemic policies with regard to vaccinations, remote work, and communicating post-pandemic changes to employees.

Remote work and leave of absence issues will likely spawn new types of workplace claims as employers navigate the "new normal" and a variety of novel workplace challenges. From claims alleging failure to accommodate workers impacted by the virus, to unsafe workplace allegations, to disputes regarding compensable work time and work-related expenses, the pandemic has given rise to an array of new workplace considerations.

"It is a common quip among employment lawyers that we are needed in both good times and bad. And that has never proven more true than during the COVID-19 pandemic," says Mark Goldstein, a partner in Reed Smith's labor and employment group. "A wide array of new workplace-related issues has arisen since March 2020, from an employer's ability to mandate that its workers be vaccinated to timekeeping and pay practices for employees who work in a remote environment. Likewise, we have seen an unprecedented number of workforce reduction programs over the past 18+ months, including both furloughs and terminations. This has resulted in a myriad of concerns, including with respect to federal and state WARN acts."

In addition, with employees in unprecedented numbers working in a hybrid or remote capacity, wage and hour claims will likely be on the rise. Employers will seek guidance on how to minimize minimum wage violations by complying with applicable laws and how to supervise employees in a remote/hybrid environment. In addition, COVID-related employment claims such as retaliation, discrimination, harassment, whistleblower actions, and claims under the Family Medical Leave Act are likely to spike in the aftermath of the pandemic.

At the same time, the US has witnessed an expansion of protected employee classes in recent years. A landmark Supreme Court ruling[4] that Title VII of the Civil Rights Acts of 1964 covers sexual orientation and transgender status, for instance, has fueled litigation asserting gender identity and sexual orientation discrimination, harassment, and other legal claims.

Moving forward, "employment lawyers are crucial as businesses evolve in light of the lessons learned from COVID-19 and adapt their workplaces to changing workplace needs, expectations, and requirements," Goldstein says.

Private equity

The private equity market, and in turn the demand for counsel, is well-positioned for growth through the balance of 2021 and well beyond. Private equity fundraising remained strong during the pandemic and through the second quarter of 2021. According to a recent Harvard University report,[5] private equity-backed buyouts comprised approximately 17 percent of overall merger and acquisition activity in 2020. Experts predict[6] that worldwide private equity assets under management will reach $5.8 trillion by 2025.

Special-purpose acquisition companies (SPACs) exploded in 2020, further fueling the need for counsel. A special-purpose acquisitions company is a shell corporation created to raise money through an IPO with the purpose of acquiring a private company. More than 200 SPACs launched in 2020,[7] with many targets in the tech, healthcare, and clean-energy sectors. Private equity firms served both as deal sponsors and as sellers. SPACs boomed again in early 2021, with a record 274 new companies listed in the first quarter. SPACs raised more than $80 billion during the first half of 2021.[8]

Private equity counsel will continue to assist firms after the pandemic with an array of challenges, including formation of private equity funds, and transactions including:

- Platform acquisitions and exits;
- Minority and majority investments;
- Add-on acquisitions;
- Outside general counsel to portfolio companies;
- Management team representations;
- Recapitalizations;
- GP buyouts/secondary transactions;
- Co-investments; and
- Going private transactions.

Given these trends, private equity is expected to continue to be an in-demand law practice area post-pandemic.

Regulatory and compliance

Regulatory frameworks are fast-changing in today's global economy and are of increasing importance to many sensitive industries. With heightened risks associated with non-compliance and growing pressure from regulatory bodies, companies seek counsel to assist with navigating complex bodies of national, state, and local regulations. This was certainly the case during the height of the pandemic, with myriad public health regulations issued and revised on a continuing basis, the enactment of the Coronavirus Aid, Relief, and Economic Security (CARES) Act, the Paycheck Protection Program, and Health Care Enhancement Act, the Coronavirus Preparedness and Response Supplemental Appropriations Act 2020, and the Families First Coronavirus Response Act. This is expected to remain true for the foreseeable future, as companies continue to seek to comply with a wide variety of existing and new regulations in a world grappling with growing threats in China, Russia, and other nations.

Companies will continue to seek counsel post-pandemic on an array of issues, including:

- **International trade** – including cross-border opportunities and commercial relationships, export controls, and economic sanctions;

- **Supply chain security** – including compliance with a series of executive orders designed to strengthen national security and US supply chain in energy, technology, infrastructure, and other industries;
- **Employment and benefits** – including employee health screenings/tests, workplace safety and reporting, remote work considerations, and discrimination issues;
- **Corporate** – including provisions in existing and new agreements that may be impacted by current and new outbreaks;
- **Real estate** – including property redesign and operations, lease amendments, and tenant changed operation;
- **Liability mitigation** – including premises liability and privacy considerations; and
- **Communications plans** – including policies and plans to keep employees and invitees safe and to confront current and new outbreaks.

"The pandemic resulted in numerous facility closures and manufacturing limitations, forcing many companies to pivot and find new producers, suppliers, distributors, and other key business relationships," states Sarah Wronsky, an attorney in Reed Smith's International Trade and National Security Group, who provides guidance to clients worldwide on issues related to international trade and regulatory enforcement matters. "As the economy reopens post-pandemic, companies must balance their reentry into the global economy with the evolving landscape in foreign trade and supply chain regulations."

Intellectual property

The demand for intellectual property counsel surged during the peak of the pandemic with the advent of COVID-19 vaccines and treatments. Healthcare innovation, in fact, topped patenting activity in 2020. Digital technologies are also fueling growth in patent filings, which reflects its central role in the digital revolution that is infiltrating all industries. With so much patent activity concerning new technology, patent disputes are inevitable. Patent and trademark related issues are sure to increase in the coming years.

"If courts follow South Africa and Australia's lead in recognizing artificial intelligence as an inventor, the increase in software patent filings will only accelerate," Christine Morgan, an intellectual property lawyer at Reed

Smith, notes. "With much of the world's business and leisure activity occurring online in the wake of COVID-19 related lockdowns, we can expect an increase in the number of patent lawsuits by owners of software patents."

The number of trademark applications filed in the third quarter of 2020 increased by more than 6,000 from the third quarter of 2019. The number of patent applications in the US has held steady since the start of the pandemic – which could be a function of the incentives created by the US Patent and Trademark Office that encourage COVID-19-related innovations.

A steady stream of anticipated new patent and trademark applications and attendant disputes will keep intellectual property a cutting-edge and hot practice area post-pandemic.

Health law

As the pandemic reshapes the delivery of health services, individuals and organizations will have a continuing need for counseling on a variety of health care-related issues, new regulations, and risk management measures. An aging global population, private equity investment, industry consolidation, the move toward personalized medicine, and the digitization of health services will also fuel growth in this practice area.

Technology will increasingly play a role in many areas, including in virtual care and telehealth, the digitizing of clinical trials, the use of data to provide personalized health care services and products, and in the development of value-based care models. With these changes, market participants will need to navigate reimbursement issues and regulatory changes, while increasingly focusing on data use, compliance, and protection.

"Never before has technology been so prevalent in the health care and life sciences sector," notes Scot Hasselman, a Reed Smith partner and co-chair of the firm's life sciences health industry group. "COVID-19 accelerated the demand for new and expanded uses in the provision of health care services, and the development of vaccines, rapid testing, lab services, and drug therapies. This expansive growth in the health care and technology space, and even the blurring of distinct lines between health care and technology, will continue for the foreseeable future."

One of the primary uses of technology in the industry is in the development of personalized medicine, including in the fields of diagnostics, therapeutics, medical care, and nutrition and wellness. Many of these new products and services will require legal counsel on FDA regulatory approvals and pathways, pricing and reimbursement, IP considerations, advertising and marketing, and other services.

Experts also expect a surge of health care enforcement and litigation in the coming year, including claims filed under various health care statutes including, in the US, the False Claims Act, the Anti-Kickback Statute, the Stark Law, and the new Interoperability rules; and, in the EU, the EU whistleblower directive, amendments to the EU Product Liability Directive, and the EU law on class action lawsuits, many of which will have significant implications for multinational and global pharmaceutical and medical device manufacturers, though not inherently industry-specific.

Finally, the health care industry represents a significant area of growth for private equity investors. Of particular interest are US healthcare providers and internationally headquartered start-up medical device, pharmaceutical, and digital health companies looking to enter the market. This increasing investment into the industry will result in a growing need for legal services in the transactional, due diligence, and financing arenas, with clients predominantly turning to counsel with specialized health care experience.

References

1. American Bar Association: www.americanbar.org/news/abanews/aba-news-archives/2021/04/new-aba-survey-outlines-employers-best-practices-for-post-pandem/
2. Lex Machina: Federal District Court – cases. Showing 3,321 federal district court cases; with General: COVID-19 case tag; filed between 2021-01-01 and 2021-07-31; sorted by most recent docket activity.
3. Insurance Information Institute: www.iii.org/publications/insurance-handbook/introduction/insurance-industry-at-a-glance
4. Squire Patton Boggs: Landmark US Supreme Court Ruling Prohibits Sexual Orientation And Gender Identity-Based Discrimination In Employment (US): www.employmentlawworldview.com/landmark-u-s-supreme-court-ruling-prohibits-sexual-orientation-and-gender-identity-based-discrimination-in-employment-us/
5. Harvard University: Private Equity – Year in Review and 2021 Outlook: https://corpgov.law.harvard.edu/2021/02/06/private-equity-year-in-review-and-2021-outlook/
6. Deloitte: The growing private equity market: How PE firms can use expertise, technology, and agility to exceed stakeholder expectations: www2.deloitte.com/us/en/insights/industry/financial-services/private-equity-industry-forecast.html
7. S&P Global: Year of the SPAC: www.spglobal.com/en/research-insights/featured/spac
8. PWC: Demand for tech capabilities and capital availability intensifies competition among corporate, private equity and SPAC buyers, raising the stakes on value-creating deals: www.pwc.com/gx/en/news-room/press-releases/2021/global-m-and-a-industry-trends-july-2021.html

Chapter 11: A happy, profitable law firm – no, really

By Debbie Epstein Henry, founder, DEH Consulting, Speaking, Writing

Introduction

As lawyers emerge from the cloak of COVID-19, when their home and work lives seemingly became one, they will seek to incorporate the learnings of the pandemic into their new work worlds. Winning law firms will be those who can build the benefits of flexible work into happier and more productive and profitable environments.

That's why I've become increasingly troubled as I've watched the latest frenzy of associate salary inflation among law firms. I'm not worried about whether the firms will be able to afford the associates' raises or whether clients will continue to pay firms' escalating rates. Nor is my concern due to naivete. I know that competition for top talent is fiercer than ever and that there's a dearth of quality associates available to do the demanding work. The crux of my worry is that heightened law firm expenses will further erode law firm culture and create an ever more intense focus on delivering maximum billable hours at the expense of the quality of lawyers' lives.

My worry is compounded by disappointment. It looks like law firms have already forgotten the valuable learnings we gained from the lockdowns. Those learnings, in essence, are that firms can be profitable and productive while also being flexible and giving lawyers more control in the way they work. Lawyers are the greatest assets of their firms yet it appears that firms still fail to understand what inspires their talent. If the lessons from the pandemic were taken to heart, firms would make flexibility, control, and quality of life integral to how they recruit and retain their talent. Instead, money is still the key lever.

To me, this means that law firms have yet to learn that building a profitable firm also requires building a happy one. Here are my six tips on what lawyers really want and how firms can seek profitability and productivity and yes, happiness for their lawyers.

Luxuriate in the billable hour

The luxury of the billable hour is that firms generate the same revenue wherever their lawyers bill. Yet even after conditions mandated remote work at many firms for more than a year, the macho pull to return onsite to the office is still strong. Let me be clear. I agree there is real value to being together in-person. The benefit of impromptu brainstorming and connection when colleagues are with each other in person is important. Yet there is nothing magical about a five-day onsite work week. We live in a customized world and the younger generation, in particular, expect that work schedules should similarly be customized. Many law firms are fearful of responding to their firms' survey feedback where lawyers articulated a preference for only two to three days onsite each week. These preferences, however, are not going away – especially now that we've seen that firms can thrive without continuous face time.

Law firms need to resist the knee-jerk default for full onsite return and instead focus on what are the most compelling factors that drive performance and results in determining lawyers' work schedules. Those factors include, most critically, the type of work lawyers do as well as their ability to perform at maximum potential and serve clients' needs most effectively. Giving lawyers more control in the way they work should generally elevate, not negatively impact, performance.

Much of this is not new. Many lawyers were already used to not seeing each other regularly pre-pandemic. The law firm lawyers who work with clients are typically not together on a regular basis and even lawyers within the same firm may be geographically dispersed and not accustomed to seeing each other. In fact, many lawyers report having "seen" each other more regularly through video during the pandemic. Visibility was effectively increased when these lawyers were used to previously only communicating by telephone.

When lawyers work flexibly, what is key, along with high quality of work, is responsiveness and accessibility. By training lawyers to confirm receipt when emails and assignments are delivered, it allays clients' and assigning partners' concerns that lawyers are not available and not being conscientious about their work. Additionally, firms that value having lawyer teams work together in person or in unison can establish core hours where certain days/hours per week are set, with the expectation that all lawyers will be onsite or working during the designated hours. For firms that are adopting a hybrid model long-term, it is helpful to use standardized schedules and rotations, wherever possible. This is a way to reduce stigma and subjectivity, given that men are returning to the office at greater rates and firms need to ensure that in-office presence does not result in those onsite being staffed on a disproportionately higher number of high-profile matters.

Invest in your firm culture

More than ever, lawyers are seeking more meaning and purpose in the work they do. Lawyers also have a heightened expectation that their firms will play an integral role in environmental, social, and governance (ESG) work. If the client work at firms doesn't deliver that meaning and purpose in the ways lawyers want, they will want to participate in social impact, pro bono, and community service through their firms. Lawyers are also expecting that their firms take a position and publicly declare their support for causes that are meaningful to them. This means taking a stand on diversity, equity, and inclusion issues, as well as other social impact work. Firms can no longer sit on the sidelines – they must speak up.

Many lawyers reported feelings of isolation in working remotely. Lawyers returning to the office will likely be seeking more affinity groups, both to feel more connected to colleagues and to become more aligned with the firm and colleagues on their identity and other issues about which they care deeply. Lawyers are also yearning for a social community through work. During their remote working, many lawyers missed the casual conversations and interactions that are natural in an onsite work day. Firms that invite those opportunities for casual connections onsite through their office designs and otherwise will make their workplaces more inviting. Also, firms that host frequent social events give colleagues a chance to connect and create forums for lawyers to build the trust and bonds they need.

Some firms are reticent to invest in their culture because they view the millennial generation, in particular, to be more transient. However, firms need their work performed now and if millennials are the best ones to do it, firms need to understand that the investment in culture is worthwhile to develop quality lawyers, even if short term. Additionally, if the millennials don't stay at their firms, they still have the opportunity to be ambassadors of their firms' brands by vouching for the training, relationships, and knowledge they built while they were there. These departed lawyers will also more likely become clients if their firms take the time to invest in them and embed their culture into their skills as lawyers.

Facilitate connection and personal development

When we could not fall back on in-person connection, we learned that effective communication is more critical than ever. The leaders who ultimately inspired their teams and kept them engaged were the ones who demonstrated their vision and confidence as well as their vulnerability and willingness to listen. Part of that effective communication is being able to adjust both the messaging and means of communication based on the evolving needs of the audience. In that vein, firms should continue to survey their lawyers regularly and not only report back on the survey findings but also be responsive to the feedback that their lawyers provide.

Part of that lawyer feedback undoubtedly will be an interest in their firms investing in their development as people, not just as lawyers. That means training lawyers on effective communication – how to listen and how to impart information clearly, concisely, and persuasively. That training should also entail developing lawyers as leaders. These skills include developing executive presence, gaining sponsorship, and learning effective negotiation, as well as self-advocacy.

Create a work–life career continuum

As firms emerge from the pandemic, they need to reframe how they envision work–life issues. Many lawyers who spent more than a year working from home witnessed, participated in, and gained more knowledge about what home responsibilities truly involve. Historically, women lawyers more often availed themselves of work–life policies at law firms and, in the pandemic, women were disproportionately burdened by home and childcare responsibilities. As firms reevaluate their work–life environments, it is critical that they think more broadly in designing work–life flexibility in a gender-neutral way, across the career spectrum. This starts with reasonable hour expectations for all lawyers and allowing lawyers to create boundaries and carve out opportunities to recharge during their work weeks as well as on weekends. Establishing and updating written policies to address work–life needs is also critical. Key areas of policy focus include flexible and reduced hours, remote and hybrid work, parental leave, re-entry into the profession, phase back from parental or other temporary leaves, and phased retirement. The exercise of drafting these policies and updating them, as needed, forces consensus and enables lawyers to be able to plan and know their firms' expectations. Additionally, lawyers expect their firms will provide resources and support around childcare, eldercare, and sick care as well as mental health. These resources will engender loyalty in lawyers and instill confidence that they can do the work they need to do while they have the support.

Embrace the flexible remote lawyer

Firms have historically been reticent to welcome lawyers who sought reduced hours that did not amount to at least a 60 percent billable hour schedule. Now's the time to rid firms of that bias permanently. The pandemic demonstrated that remote lawyering is not just viable but it makes economic sense. Firms should no longer be weighing a lawyer's billable hours against his or her overhead expenses. If firms embrace a new category of lawyer without a billable hour minimum and without an office presence (the "flexible remote lawyer"), the overhead math no longer applies and instead the flexible remote lawyer simply becomes an agile talent resource to fill in for the inevitable ebb and flow of clients' needs. This elastic opportunity for law firms to expand and contract their workforces while meeting the needs of lawyers who are looking to stay engaged in the practice and earn an income without having the additional demands of full-time employees is long overdue. What's more, this becomes a means for firms to develop a pipeline of top talent that needs or wants more flexibility for an indefinite term. In turn, firms are able to maintain relationships and cultivate skills that may lead to an easier path for many of these lawyers to have a more expansive return.

Perpetuate the inventive spirit

The pandemic was a time of upheaval and it forced law firms to do things differently. It's important that firms don't lapse back into what was. Firms need to take advantage of the window of openness and continue to explore new ideas. They should institute pilots and experiment with different practice areas, methods of working, team compositions, approaches to bill clients, ways of doling out assignments, and techniques for business development, and see what is worth keeping. Also, firms need to anticipate that the transition back for many will be big. Instead of expecting a full onsite return, firms should plan for the hybrid and plan for the patchwork. They should assume that flexibility will be expected and stop calling it an accommodation. Instead, firms should see flexibility as the ability to be cutting edge in the way they attract and engage talent just as they would value being creative in developing strategies for clients or creating new practice areas for their firms. Law firms will need to evaluate and track their successes and mishaps and be willing to regroup and redirect accordingly. They should also survey their clients and ask them what they want that's different and be willing to try that too.

Conclusion

Law firms that seek a more humane means to deliver legal services with a heightened sensitivity to well-being and well-doing will improve their connection to clients as well as their engagement of lawyers. This will not only enhance law firm performance but also the lawyer experience to create happier, more successful, and more sustainable firms into the future.

About Globe Law and Business

Globe Law and Business was established in 2005. From the very beginning, we set out to create law books which are sufficiently high level to be of real use to the experienced professional, yet still accessible and easy to navigate. Most of our authors are drawn from Magic Circle and other top commercial firms, both in the UK and internationally.

Our titles are carefully produced, with the utmost attention paid to editorial, design and production processes. We hope this results in high-quality publications that are easy to read, and a pleasure to own. Our titles are also available as ebooks, which are compatible with most desktop, laptop and tablet devices. In 2018 we expanded our portfolio to include journals and Special Reports, available both digitally and in hard copy format, and produced to the same high standards as our books.

In the Spring of 2021, we were very pleased to announce the start of a new chapter for Globe Law and Business following the acquisition of law books under the imprint Ark Publishing. We are very much looking forward to working with our new Ark authors, many of whom are well-known to us, and to further developing the law firm management list, among other areas.

We'd very much like to hear from you with your thoughts and ideas for improving what we offer. Please do feel free to email me at sian@globelawandbusiness.com with your views.

Sian O'Neill
Managing director
Globe Law and Business
www.globelawandbusiness.com

www.ingramcontent.com/pod-product-compliance
Ingram Content Group UK Ltd.
Pitfield, Milton Keynes, MK11 3LW, UK
UKHW021849150926
8657IPUK00005B/153

9 781787 42801